Feminism and Gender Politics in Mediated Popular Music

Feminism and Gender Politics in Mediated Popular Music

Ann Werner

BLOOMSBURY ACADEMIC
NEW YORK • LONDON • OXFORD • NEW DELHI • SYDNEY

BLOOMSBURY ACADEMIC
Bloomsbury Publishing Inc
1385 Broadway, New York, NY 10018, USA
50 Bedford Square, London, WC1B 3DP, UK
29 Earlsfort Terrace, Dublin 2, Ireland

BLOOMSBURY, BLOOMSBURY ACADEMIC and the Diana logo are trademarks of Bloomsbury Publishing Plc

First published in the United States of America 2023
This paperback edition published 2024

Copyright © Ann Werner, 2023

For legal purposes the Acknowledgements on p. viii constitute an extension of this copyright page.

Cover image © Maskot/Getty Images

All rights reserved. No part of this publication may be reproduced or transmitted in any form or by any means, electronic or mechanical, including photocopying, recording, or any information storage or retrieval system, without prior permission in writing from the publishers.

Bloomsbury Publishing Inc does not have any control over, or responsibility for, any third-party websites referred to or in this book. All internet addresses given in this book were correct at the time of going to press. The author and publisher regret any inconvenience caused if addresses have changed or sites have ceased to exist, but can accept no responsibility for any such changes.

Library of Congress Cataloguing-in-Publication Data

Names: Werner, Ann, 1976- author.
Title: Feminism and gender politics in mediated popular music / Ann Werner.
Description: [1st.] | New York, NY : Bloomsbury Academic, 2022. | Includes bibliographical references and index. | Summary: "Addresses feminism and gender issues in mainstream mediated popular music culture, such as feminist pop artists, music industry #MeToo petitions and gender equality efforts"– Provided by publisher.
Identifiers: LCCN 2022009576 (print) | LCCN 2022009577 (ebook) | ISBN 9781501368509 (hardback) | ISBN 9781501369650 (paperback) | ISBN 9781501368516 (epub) | ISBN 9781501368523 (pdf) | ISBN 9781501368530
Subjects: LCSH: Popular music–Social aspects. | Feminism and music. | Women in the music trade. | Sex role in music. | MeToo movement.
Classification: LCC ML3918.P6 W47 2022 (print) | LCC ML3918.P6 (ebook) | DDC 306.4/8424–dc23/eng/20220307
LC record available at https://lccn.loc.gov/2022009576
LC ebook record available at https://lccn.loc.gov/2022009577

ISBN: HB: 978-1-5013-6850-9
PB: 978-1-5013-6965-0
ePDF: 978-1-5013-6852-3
eBook: 978-1-5013-6851-6

Typeset by Deanta Global Publishing Services, Chennai, India

To find out more about our authors and books visit www.bloomsbury.com and sign up for our newsletters.

Contents

List of figures	vii
Acknowledgements	viii
Introduction	**1**
Women and music, gender in music	5
More than a woman	6
Post-feminism in popular music, a feminism?	9
Gender mainstreaming and the music industries	11
Media, technology and post-humanist feminism	12
Outline of the book	14
1 Mediating the feminist superstar: Beyoncé, Lady Gaga and Taylor Swift in Netflix documentaries	**19**
Feminism, post-feminism and popular music	22
The documentaries	26
Meeting the artists	29
Achieving and moving on	36
Feminism, southern Black culture and LGBTQ+ rights	40
Conclusion	47
2 Narratives about gender and feminism in a music industry #MeToo petition	**49**
Research on #MeToo, hashtag feminism and online feminist activism	52
The stories told	55
The young survivor	57
Gendering survivors and perpetrators	61
Gender – again	65
Loving music in the workplaces of the music industries	66

	Narrating time and place	70
	Feminist demands	71
	Conclusion	74
3	**Gender equality, diversity and algorithmic culture on music streaming services**	**77**
	Algorithmic culture and feminist algorithm studies	79
	Equalizing music streaming services	81
	Analysing gender in the most-streamed songs on Spotify 2019	92
	Conclusion	104
4	**Keychange: Gender equality work in the popular music industries**	**107**
	Keychange	108
	Organizing for gender equality in popular music	111
	How it started	115
	A programme for career development	117
	Gendering the participants of the programme	121
	A pledge for gender equality	126
	A manifesto to change policy	129
	What is Keychange's solution to gender inequality in music?	131
	Conclusion	135
Conclusion		**137**
	Feminisms in popular music	138
	Mediated feminisms	141
	Gender politics	142
	Where to now?	143
References		147
Index		158

Figures

1.1 Lady Gaga ascends for her *Superbowl* half-time performance in 2017   27
1.2 Taylor Swift receives a Video of the Year Award for 'You Need to Calm Down' with some of the cast from the video at the MTV Video Music Awards in 2019   39
1.3 Beyoncé performs 'Crazy in Love' with a large brass band at the Coachella Valley Music and Arts Festival in 2018   41
3.1 Lil Nas X eats chicken wings at the 'Old Town Road' premiere party in 2019 wearing one of his outfits from the music video   99
3.2 Billie Eilish speaks onstage at the LACMA Art + Film Gala in 2019 with green highlights in her hair and a loose-fitting Gucci shirt   102
4.1 The term 'gender minority' as explained on the Keychange.eu website in 2021   120
4.2 Keychange is presented as a movement with words and a photo on the Keychange.eu website in 2021   122
4.3 What Keychange is as explained on the PRS Foundation's website, prsfoundation.com, in 2021   124
4.4 What Keychange is as explained on the Musikcentrum Öst's website, musikcentrumost.se, in 2021   125
4.5 What Keychange is as explained on the Reeperbahn Festival website, reeperbahnfestival.com, in 2021   132

Acknowledgements

The idea to write this book came about after speaking at the symposium 'Exploring Gender Dynamics in the Music Industry' at the University of Groningen, the Netherlands, in May 2019. I would like to thank all participants, especially the organizer Kristin McGee for inviting me and for the conversations we shared. The event and the discussions made me see that feminist ideas brought changes to the music industries during the 2010s. Attending the symposium with music industry representatives and scholars roused a curiosity to investigate how feminism had entered the music industries and what (if anything) had really changed. The book was then made possible by the editorial team at Bloomsbury: Leah Babb-Rosenfeld and Rachel Moore, their ideas, support and patience. I also want to thank the three anonymous reviewers who helped me shape a better book than I had first imagined I could write. Thank you!

Receiving a PUSH grant from Södertörn University, Sweden, in collaboration with Vinnova enabled me to do archive studies of #MeToo petitions at Svenskt visarkiv and I am thankful for my time there. Thanks to Mischa van Kaan and his colleagues who helped me. Sadly, my stay was cut short because of the pandemic. I would also like to thank Academic Rights Press and their service Music Industry Data for providing me with access to the Spotify data I used to analyse the most-streamed songs. Ragnar Berthling and Mia Ternström from Musikcentrum Öst and Keychange made the chapter about Keychange possible by providing me with their time and knowledge, and also reading the draft chapter.

During the writing process, I had much help from my colleagues at Gender Studies and adjoining departments at Södertörn University, who read and discussed draft chapters of the book at our advanced seminars. Thanks to everyone who came to these seminars and read my texts. A special thanks to Jenny Sundén who helped me see what book writing is all about, from the proposal to the finished product. I would also like to thank colleagues outside

Södertörn University who gave me feedback on chapter drafts during the time of writing: Anna Lundberg, Anna Adeniji and Tami Gadir. I would like to thank Sam de Boise for showing me the Smirnoff equalizer, and a musician friend who gave me important insights into the Swedish #MeToo movement. Finally, and most importantly, I want to thank my family: Krish, Mahina and my mother.

Introduction

Saweetie and Doja Cat are lying on sunbeds tanning and drinking mimosas in spectacular bikinis when they are approached by a man. In the opening scene of the music video for the rap song 'Best friend' (2021), the man says, 'I can't believe these disrespectful men out here, just staring at y'all bodies, objectifying y'all'. The statement is a critique of (hetero) pick-up culture, but there are no other men around and the man speaking is the only one staring at their bodies. His actions provoke Saweetie and Doja Cat into an imagined conversation that the man cannot hear, using the expressions 'misogynist', 'ally to the feminist cause' and 'toxic masculinity'. These also appear written in the frame of the music video. After their critique of the man, they dismiss him with a 'Bye baby' and the song starts. In the lyrics, they go on to celebrate each other and female friendship with the chorus 'That's my best friend, she a real bad bitch'. The best friend (both of the artists) is described as having her own money, her own car, she knows how to tip in a strip club, twerk, she can protect and attack and has been around (for her friend) since childhood. The music video is ridiculing the man trying to pick up Saweetie and Doja Cat, positioning the artists as part of 'the feminist cause'. The song includes messages of female financial independence and physical strength. Simultaneously, the rappers are showing off a lot of skin, fancy outfits, ass-shaking dance moves and a tough attitude. The music video is in alliance with the beauty industry by portraying nice clothes, accessories and make-up, *and* is encouraging feminist resistance to sexism, painting a picture of the contemporary female artist as political, in solidarity and resistant, beautiful and desirable. 'Best friend' is depicting both feminism and a commodification of the gender performances of the artists.

Feminist politics is not typically associated with mainstream popular music. Not so long ago, an overt use of feminist vocabulary would have been surprising in a rap song with female artists in sexy outfits; however, in 2021 feminist discourse has become integrated in chart-climbing popular music and is unsurprising. Calling oneself a feminist, or expressing support for women's rights, and discussing the sexism of the music industries are now easily combined with being a sexy, trendy and successful pop artist. Denouncing feminist issues may prove more difficult for a female artist in the current climate of internationally successful mainstream popular music.

This book discusses the way feminism and gender politics have been articulated in mediated popular music during the second half of the 2010s. Already in the 1990s, scholars acknowledged that thematic interpretations of feminist issues, women pursuing careers in male-dominated fields such as law and the police, women juggling love, family and work, had entered popular culture (Tasker & Negra 2007). In the 2010s, the word 'feminism' and the vocabulary associated with feminist activist politics stopped being taboo in popular culture and the media (Rottenberg 2018). In popular music critiques of gender inequality, and support for feminist activism can be seen in artists' practices, expressed in lyrics, music and performances, and in the gender equality work of the music industries. Examples include Beyoncé performing 'Flawless' on stage in front of the word 'feminist'; #MeToo petitions in the music industry all over the world; the documentaries *Surviving R Kelly* and *On the Record*; songs and performances critiquing and transforming sexist gender stereotypes by M.I.A., Lady Gaga, Nicki Minaj and Janelle Monáe; music-focused activist networks such as female:pressure; and musical feminist flash mob protests like 'un violador en tu camino'. Previously, the Riot Grrrl movement had been *the* widely known feminist popular music movement (Leonard 2007, Bock 2008), with 'girl power's' entrance into popular music by the Spice Girls and other chart-topping artists following suit as a commercial appropriation of Riot Grrrl (Banet-Weiser 2018, Schilt 2003).

The meanings of feminism and gender politics in mediated popular music are not easy to grasp. It is no longer a handful artists in the mainstream who call themselves feminist, or explicitly address issues facing women: sexual violence, domestic violence, career challenges or economic inequality, lack of reproductive rights, etc. Contradictions also endure; sexism, discrimination, exclusion and sexual harassment are still commonplace both in artist experiences, fan cultures and the lyrical content of popular music (see for example Coleman 2017, Hill 2016, Müller 2017). And the numerical representation of women-identified artists, writers and producers in popular music is still low (Bain 2019, Smith et al. 2021). While it is possible to be a feminist in popular music, there is still gendered oppression in the music industries that call for feminist work. The song by Saweetie and Doja Cat that served as an opening example in this book is produced by Dr Luke, who is also credited as one of the (seven) writers of 'Best friend'. Dr Luke became a household name when artist Kesha sued him for physical, sexual and emotional abuse in 2014 – a few years before #MeToo. And even though he was never convicted, several artists have taken a public stand against him due to his working methods. Feminism in mediated popular music is not simply a story of progress, where music is becoming more feminist, or a narrative where we can identify the good guys and the villains, when the producer of a feminist rap song is also an (alleged) abuser. Feminist ideas and gender ideals are travelling through popular music and the types of feminism and gender politics performed are multidimensional, some radical, some liberal or post-feminist, some allying themselves with anti-racism and lesbian, gay, bisexual, trans*, queer and more (LGBTQ+) rights. This development coexists with the growth of social media and the algorithmic culture of streaming services that are mediating stories about gender, feminism and popular music in new ways.

Feminist ideas influence popular music, and ideals of masculinities and femininities are played out at the same time as politically charged gender representations. In this volume, feminism(s) taking place in popular music is investigated through four examples: in documentaries by well-known artists; music industry #MeToo activism; music streaming services, marketing and charts; and in a gender equality project for people working in music. Throughout the four chapters, the aim is to identify what kind of feminisms are present in mediated popular music and what kind of gender politics those feminisms bring with them. Questions asked include: How are feminist views formulated in popular music? How is gender equality and gender oppression described? What solutions are presented? What gendered ideals are present in feminist popular music?

The starting point of this volume is that mediated popular culture is a rich field for studying the meaning of gender, sexuality, race and class in contemporary society through representation (Hall 1997). Here, representations of gender are seen as discursively constructed in popular music *and* as materially embedded. The ideas about gender represented in popular music carry significance. Elizabeth Grosz (1995: 18) formulates the gendering process in culture as a complex relation between the corporeality of the author, texts' materiality and its effects in marking the bodies of the author and the readers. With this definition, mediated popular music is symbolic, shaped by discourse, but embedded in the embodiment of those producing and those listening, and the media technology used to do so. Feminism and gender politics are being shaped and constructed by symbolic and material processes subject to change.

The case studies in this book are political because they aim to change the music industries and the world, to make it more equal, drawing on ideological arguments. Developments in media technology such as the rise of social media and streaming services interplay with feminism and gender politics in the content and style of popular music. For example, social media has allowed artists to take over the mediation of their artist personas from tabloid magazines and television, and social media (Facebook and Twitter) provided sites for feminist media activism in the #MeToo movement by their potential for connectivity and viral spreading of messages. The popularity of feminism and gender politics in popular music has grown in the mediatized society of the 2010s. This book aims therefore to revitalize the discussion on media representations of feminism, gender and gender equality in popular music.[1] Feminism as expressed in mediated popular music is in dialogue with contemporary feminist theoretical discussions described in this introduction: a feminist critique of musical canon and the underrepresentation of women, intersectionality, queer theory, post-feminism, gender mainstreaming and post-humanist feminist understandings of media and technology.

---

[1] Popular music is here understood as music that is popular with or listened to by many, mass distributed and follows defined aesthetic ideals of genre, time and context (Shuker 2017: 265–6). The purpose here is not to challenge or debate the concept 'popular music', it makes up the empirical field of the book exemplified in the four cases.

Women and music, gender in music

What traditions, political and theoretical, are popular music artists following when they are calling themselves feminists, or addressing women's rights, gender inequality, misogyny, sexism, sexual violence and sexual harassment in the music industries today? Research on women, gender and feminism in music is a vibrant field that is growing and changing in conversation with feminist theoretical debates. Feminist scholarly discussions about the lack of women in the curriculum, for example in music history, has led feminist researchers to write about 'women in music', aiming to bring forward knowledge about these women, for example female composers (e.g. Hamer 2021). The critique of musical canon as masculine and gendered, and the scholarly work to add women to the canon of different music traditions are two approaches attempting to answer the question about why there is continued under-representation of women in most types of music practice. The under-representation of women, and trans people,[2] is clearly affecting popular music (Smith et al. 2021). Striving to include women to promote gender equality in numbers requires that the gendered make-up of producers, artists and composers is questioned, since male dominance colours the popular music industries today, rarely putting women above 20 per cent (Smith et al. 2021). The liberal feminist idea behind such reasoning is that if women access the arena (music) in the same numbers as men, gender equality will follow. A liberal feminist political stance is signified by focusing on rights and inclusion for women, arguing everyone's equal worth. The category of women may be taken for granted as a biological category, but liberal feminism more commonly understands 'gender' as socially constructed.

This empiricist or practical approach to women and music also gave rise to a different critique of music itself. In music history, musicology and music education, scholars investigating canons, curricula and teaching methods

---

[2] Trans people's representation has not been mapped as often as women's representation in popular music and other cultural industries. It is still important to highlight that gender is not a binary category in contemporary popular music or contemporary feminist theory.

from a feminist perspective have critiqued gender as not a pregiven category (Green 1997). A critical deconstruction of the canon in classical music by Marcia J. Citron (1993: 136) discusses not only that the canon is masculine, but also how ideas about gender and musical forms, like a sonata, shape the valuing and categorization of music in terms of gender (e.g. McClary 1991). Thus, the problem is not that women's physical presence is missing in musical institutions and practices, but that musical quality has been constructed and valued in terms that are gendered. According to Citron, qualities constructed as masculine have been valued higher in modernity and in Western music traditions. With such an outlook, it is not sufficient to 'add women', the canon, curricula and value systems of music must be deconstructed and questioned using a feminist critique of power.

More than a woman

There has been a long-standing critique in feminist theory and politics of seeing 'woman' as a unified category where all 'women' need the same political change, where gender is binary with two options: male/female. How to turn away from an 'add women' approach and question the (feminist) results of such assumptions for research have been debated in feminist theory. Intersectionality, a widely discussed and conceptual solution has been proposed by Black US feminists (Crenshaw 1991, Collins 1998) to keep talking about 'women' without making it a unified category. Intersectionality is an analytical tool and a political feminist strategy, approaching gender as always already constructed in relation to other sociocultural categories like class, race, functionality, sexuality, ethnicity, religion and so on (Lykke 2010: 50). Intersectionality can be defined as the interaction of several power trajectories, originally gender, class and race in the formulation of the concept by Kimberlé Crenshaw (1991), and how they affect the social and cultural life of individuals and groups. Many contemporary feminist scholars agree that gender must be understood in interplay with other categorizations (Lykke 2010: 52), and that feminism must look to oppressions other than gender oppression. Crenshaw (1991) argued that structural intersectionality is the process by which intersecting power dimensions structure society, and political intersectionality is when political strategies take intersecting power trajectories into account in working for social change. Scholars using the concept of intersectionality are not the only feminist scholars arguing that gender must be understood in interplay with other categorizations. Introduced in the late 1980s, queer theory is another influential theoretical movement in feminist studies arguing for the centrality of the construction of (white) heterosexuality in gendered culture and society (Butler 1990, de Lauretis 1987). Queer theory deconstructs the subject of feminist studies in a post-structuralist vein and is fundamentally different ontologically from some applications of intersectional feminist thinking that may be realist. The interplay between gender and several other sociocultural categorizations is central in queer theory while the theorization of heterosexuality and normativity is the main contribution.

Today, intersectional approaches to gender are based on several feminist theoretical strands, including queer theory. 'Intersectional' meaning more than just gender has taken hold as a perspective in research on gender and popular music: analysing *only* gender in popular music is no longer as common (e.g. Hawkins 2017). During the same period, political intersectionality has influenced feminist movements in music. Racism and LGBTQ+ rights are issues raised by artists who are also describing themselves as feminist. This is illustrated in Susan Fast and Craig Jennex's (2019) recent book on queer and feminist interventions in popular music where 'whiteness', 'difference' and 'decolonization' are the themes of the first three parts, but 'feminism' and 'queer', although used in the title of the book, are not themes of their own. Feminism in popular music practice and research has come to include discussion on equality for several groups, the use of multiple sociocultural categorizations and discussions of multiple power trajectories, not a singular 'woman'.

Feminism and gender politics are concepts and topics in focus for this volume. But as has been shown, the political and theoretical discussions about feminism and gender cannot be fully separated from other social justice movements and other sociocultural categories. In the late 2010s, the interlinkages of social justice movements have been significant. When Saweetie and Doja Cat are drawing on feminist discourse in 'Best friend', their use of the word 'woke' and other African-American vernacular expressions also connotes Black US contemporary culture and anti-racism. In Black US culture, resistance to racism and class oppression has been expressed in rap music and the hip-hop culture. Therefore, it is relevant to ask if Saweetie and Doja Cat should be understood as feminist? Or rather as Black US feminists? Or even as Black US hip-hop feminists (Durham 2014)? Addressing issues such as the criminalization of African-American communities in the United States – one scene in the music video shows the artists taking mug shots with each other's names tattooed on their faces – and Black heterosexual masculinity as playing out in pick-up culture makes them more than just women. Using an intersectional approach requires feminism and gender politics to be analysed together with race, nation and other sociocultural categorizations.

A prominent field of research on music and gender in the 2000's are studies of how gender, femininities and masculinities are often but not always articulated in relation to other sociocultural categories in popular music. Research on gender and popular music has been concerned with visual and textual representations in genres like rock (Kearney 2017) where gender and class have been examined, and in scholarly studies of influential female artists like Madonna, Tori Amos and Beyoncé (Whiteley 2000; 2005, Burns 2002, Trier-Bieniek 2016), also investigating sexuality, race and more. This book builds on traditions from previous research on gender and popular music where gendered power is seen as a field of tension expressed in media. One early example of such work is by Lisa A. Lewis (1990) who discusses the contradictory gender politics of MTV during the 1980s, noting that the then new media format of the music video, and the television channel MTV, opened up possibilities for playful gender performances by female artists like Tina Turner and Madonna. But MTV also opened avenues for sexism and racism and was largely dominated by representations of white masculinity. This tension where gendered popular music can be seen as both empowering *and* limiting for female and feminist artists and audiences holds relevance today. In scholarship concerned with audiences and practitioners' uses of popular music, Mavis Bayton (1998) studied the possibilities and limitations for female rock musicians ethnographically and saw them gendering rock, negotiating a genre-coded masculinity and performing a balancing act for female rock musicians, located in a certain national, genre and gendered context. A large field explored in popular music studies and adjoining fields are ethnographic and audience studies of listeners, fans and artists' gendered sense of popular music, including their own perceptions of their identity formation of gender, sexuality, class, age and race (e.g. Baker 2004, Farrugia & Hay 2020, Taylor 2012). All these examples additionally illustrate how 'gender' in contemporary scholarship about gender and popular music is studied as interconnected with other power trajectories.

Post-feminism in popular music, a feminism?

The growing presence of women and girls in cultural representations took hold during the 1990s, but had begun earlier than that, and the changing way they were portrayed as taking active roles as rock stars and career women, was labelled a post-feminist cultural condition (McRobbie 2009). Feminist issues were being raised in popular culture and female leads were included, but without mentioning feminism or addressing global structural inequalities of gender, race and class. In popular music, one prominent example was the Spice Girls and their branding of the term 'girl power' (Leonard 2007, Banet-Weiser 2018). The Spice Girls' feminist intentions were performed as 'girl power', presenting themselves as young, feminine and powerful: ready to conquer the world. Their political authenticity was questioned in the 1990s and the group has been discussed as a commodification of feminism where ideas with feminist origins are simplified and used to sell goods. Scholars have argued that while audiences may indeed be empowered by the Spice Girls' message then and now, the group was commodifying feminism (Schilt 2003: 14) and simplifying and individualizing feminist issues and gender inequality in the process. Individualizing feminist issues by using feminist ideas like 'empowerment' and 'independence' to brand products (Lieb 2013), reducing freedom to the freedom to have hairy armpits (or not), is a tendency of a larger neoliberal context colouring contemporary popular music (James 2015). Neoliberal capitalism is signified by the marketization and individualization of everything, from policy to person, from higher education to hip hop. Robin James (2020: 5) has accounted for the influence of post-feminist sentiments on popular music and describes how feminist ideas of empowerment, sex and body positivity and self-confidence took over the US charts in 2014 with Meghan Trainor, Nicki Minaj, Taylor Swift and Demi Lovato establishing popular music as a place for feminist messages.

Post-feminism and the spectrum of the popularization of feminist ideas related to it have three things in common: a positive emotional outlook, a focus on individualistic feminist action and a display of feminist statements and views (not necessarily leading to more than the display itself). James (2020) argues that these post-feminist traits can be found in popular music. Being angry or sad or impoverished by gender inequality and other inequalities or doing collective, difficult and slow work to achieve social change in policy, economy or politics is not what a post-feminist sensibility is about. It builds on feminism as self-confidence, resilience and a positive mental attitude (Gill 2017), much like the Spice Girls. The popularization of feminism in popular culture, and in popular music, has rightly been critiqued for being part of a market economy where feminist ideas are used to sell anything from music to deodorants.

A consequence of the academic critique of post-feminist culture and media is a hierarchization of feminisms. While this is not the intention of any single scholar, the discussion about how feminist messages have been taking hold in popular culture from the 1990s onwards describes the popularization of feminism in negative terms. Popular feminisms become lesser feminisms. This line of thinking, lesser feminisms as opposed to authentic feminisms, has also been articulated in media debates about the feminism of popular music artists. Taylor Swift and Beyoncé, both discussed in Chapter 1, have been called feminists as well as fake-feminists. Performing the right type of feminism seems difficult for these artists. Feminism can be defined (simply) as the struggle for gender-based oppressions to stop, acknowledging that gender oppression interacts with other forms of oppression (hooks 1984). Feminism has resulted in political movements fighting for equal pay, voting rights and reproductive rights, consent, divorce and not to be murdered, harassed or assaulted because of your gender (including trans and non-binary people). Ontological understandings of what gender is, as well epistemological understandings about how knowledge about gender should be obtained and political understandings about what should be done to end gender oppression vary largely within feminism. Therefore, I ague, post-feminist feminism in popular music is a valid variation of feminism with strengths and weaknesses. Individualization and marketization in line with neoliberal capitalism are well-established weaknesses in post-feminism, but its ability to bring feminist issues to large audiences – potentially touching them and changing their lives – should be considered a strength.

Gender mainstreaming and the music industries

During the same period as the rise of post-feminism, gender mainstreaming has taken hold in the music industries. In the recording industry, the live music industry and music streaming industry, ideas based on gender mainstreaming are present (Raine & Strong 2019, Wolfe 2020). Gender mainstreaming is an internationally adopted strategy for promoting gender equality that involves integrating a gender perspective into the preparation, design, implementation, monitoring and evaluation of policies, regulatory measures and spending programmes.[3] Gender mainstreaming has been widely adopted in the European Union, advocated for by United Nations Women and implemented by non-governmental organizations around the world. The idea behind gender mainstreaming is that gender equality should be implemented at all levels of organizations, and the methods used are diverse (Prügl 2011). This notion challenges previous types of gender equality work implementing 'women's projects' that are not integrated in day-to-day practice. Gender mainstreaming methods aim to include women in decision-making, question the gender inequality mechanisms of organizations and sometimes rebuild whole organizations and businesses to be more equal (Squires 2005).[4]

---

[3] https://eige.europa.eu/gender-mainstreaming/what-is-gender-mainstreaming (accessed 1 February 2022).
[4] The concept 'women' is problematized in some gender mainstreaming work. But holding on to the idea of women and men as binary categories is common in gender mainstreaming.

In feminist scholarship, the merits of gender mainstreaming strategies have been the subject of heated discussions. Gender mainstreaming has been accused of becoming just a performance of gender equality (putting some women in power positions as tokens) rather than sincere work towards social equality for all, or a challenge to systems of power. Judith Squires (2005: 384) argues that gender mainstreaming may amount to simply 'add women' and that this aim is trapped in a liberal egalitarian approach to equality that limits impact by not addressing structural and cultural problems. In her view, liberal egalitarian feminism would pursue simple measures for gender equality. Believing that all people have the same starting position makes 'adding women' an easy solution to gender inequality. Here, echoing the attempts to add women to music history discussed above. Sam de Boise (2019: 127) argues that gender mainstreaming in the music industries tends to focus on exactly that, including women by putting a larger number of them on stage. By doing so, de Boise writes (ibid.), gender's intersections with other sociocultural categories and other types of music participation (of audiences, artists and repertoire (A&R) agents and record company bosses to name a few) are obscured. Without always using the term, the approach of gender mainstreaming work that aims to add women has gained popularity and coloured discussions about gender equality in popular music. Educating and integrating women, trans- and non-binary people in the practices of music are presented as a solution to under-representation (Björck 2011). As Squires (2005) notes, there is no proof that this approach will change the power dynamics in the music industries or any other organizations. Nevertheless, she also argues that gender mainstreaming can be transformative if it succeeds in addressing all parts of an organization, structural and cultural, to promote equality.

Media, technology and post-humanist feminism

Mediatization and technological development have changed culture and society with the introduction of social media, smartphones, streaming services and internet video sharing sites. These devices and services have greatly affected popular music's production, distribution and consumption.

Media development has enabled new forms of visibility for artists. Carol Vernallis (2013: 181) has argued that the music video format was transformed and reborn on YouTube by feminist artists like Beyoncé and Lady Gaga who incorporated the humour and vitality of DIY YouTube culture in their music videos. The technological advancements in popular music mean that new technology continues to interplay with the gendering of popular music work; for example, in the experiences of female producers working in male-dominated studios (Wolfe 2020).

In feminist theory, changing media technology and heightened debates about the sustainability of the Anthropocene way of life are met with renewed interest for materiality: technology, nature, body/affect and animals. In discussing the theoretical contribution of critical post-humanism, Rosi Braidotti (2019) has argued that the core of critical post-humanist perspectives is neo-materialist approaches to environmental, socio-economic and affective ecologies of belonging (such as gender, race, sexuality and class). Using neo-materialist ontologies suggests that the material dimensions of culture and society matter as such and are not only inscribed in discourse and representation or predestined to play the part intended by their human makers. Neo-material feminisms are influenced by previous work in feminist science and technology studies by scholars such as Donna Haraway (1991) and Katherine Hayles (1999) who argue that the human is already interconnected with technology, there is no binary between the human and the machine and that this interconnection is also gendered. In post-humanist feminism, the borders of the human are further questioned in relation to nature, animals and technology including digital media (Sundén 2015). In research on gender, feminism and popular music, post-humanist or neo-materialist approaches have, for example, been employed to understand how voices are gendered in material, discursive, aesthetic and political processes (Muchitsch 2020), and how environmental politics and the relation to nature is influencing contemporary popular music feminism (Susdorf 2017). Post-humanist feminist perspectives on popular music complement the analysis of gendered music discourse in the media (Coates 1998, Leonard 2007, Hill 2016) by using a different ontological perspective. Seeing music and media technology as meaningful in itself and as part of a gendered popular music culture.

Outline of the book

The four empirical chapters that follow the introduction answer the questions posed here by analysing US feminist popular music superstars' Netflix-released documentaries and narratives about sexual harassment and sexual violence in a #MeToo petition from Sweden. Streaming services' gender equality and diversity efforts are placed in relation to the gendering of popular music on Spotify's most-streamed lists in four countries, and Keychange, a European gender equality project aiming to overcome barriers for women and minority genders in the music industries is investigated. The cases were chosen to shed light on the recent interplay between feminism, gender politics, popular music and media culture by exemplifying current trends from production, musical content, and distribution and consumption perspectives. They draw on material from the United States and Europe familiar to the (Swedish) author, still, the examples also have international and global appeal. Spotify, #MeToo, Netflix music documentaries and gender equality work in the music industries are global phenomena even if this book cannot cover examples from all over the world.

All four chapters build on new and unique empirical research. They include an analysis of different media forms: music documentary films, social media petitions, marketing material and big data from a streaming service and websites. The #MeToo petitions were collected and shaped by social media; the documentaries were made by production companies and released on the world-dominating film and television streaming service; the marketing material of music streaming services includes social media and advertising videos; quantitative streaming data from one service is also drawn upon; the websites of the partners in Keychange are analysed; and current debates in the press about gender equality in popular music are discussed to provide context. Each chapter discusses the role of mediation and media debate in feminist popular music culture and relates to some of the feminist theoretical concepts introduced here in the introduction including liberal feminism, intersectionality, post-feminism, gender mainstreaming, post-humanism and feminist neo-materialism.

The first chapter analyses the type of feminisms represented in Netflix-released documentaries portraying feminist superstars: well-known popular music stars who call themselves feminists and have thematized feminist issues in their careers during the 2010s. Beyoncé, Lady Gaga and Taylor Swift serve as examples, chosen for their worldwide reach and appeal, and the discussion about their feminisms uses their respective Netflix-released documentaries: *Homecoming* (2019), *Gaga: Five Foot Two* (2017) and *Miss Americana* (2020) as empirical material, while also drawing on other mediated examples from their careers for context. The chapter uses concepts from the scholarly critique of post-feminist popular culture and asks if these are sufficient as analytical tools for understanding the feminist work of the three artists. In the chapter, the affective connections with audiences and other groups presented in the documentaries, when the superstars reach out to them in affective solidarity, are analysed using neo-materialist affect theory. Several feminist ideas are put forward by these stars. The chapter argues that they should be understood as artists with the potential for feminist affective change, not simply as commodified feminism.

Chapter 2 analyses sixty-four narratives about the experiences of sexual harassment and sexual violence in the music industries from a music industry #MeToo petition and the petition's editorial text accompanying them. The #MeToo petition, #NärMusikenTystnar (when the music stops), was published in Sweden's largest daily newspaper in November 2017 and mirrors problems also defined in contemporary research on sexual harassment and sexual violence in the music industries. In the context of other #MeToo petitions in music work and research on networked social media feminism, the chapter asks how gender and the music industries are constructed in the narratives of the petition and what feminist politics the demands display. The petition constructs the survivors and the signatories of the petition as gendered feminine subjects of very different sorts: young, naïve and scared versus strong, mature and decisive. The chapter also suggest paths for policy change in the music industries. The chapter concludes that the petition constructs a gendered artist who is both at risk and posing feminist demands, and that the networked self of social media used by the #MeToo movement enables such multiplicity and contradiction, a strength of the petition.

Chapter 3 analyses the Smirnoff equalizer (2018–20), an algorithmic intervention for gender equality in music listening launched by Smirnoff and Spotify, targeting gender inequality in music consumption. How can the equalizer be understood as an example of gender equality work in music streaming, and what contexts of gender representations was it speaking to? Gender mainstreaming and critiques of it are discussed to contextualize what has been done and achieved by the equalizer. Smirnoff and Spotify's gender equality initiative is compared with three other efforts for equality by music streaming services: Apple Music's #GlobalFeminism, Tidal's Path to Pride and Black Lives Matter on Spotify, Apple Music and Tidal. To understand the context of the gender equality, queer-inclusive and anti-racist efforts by music streaming services, the content of Spotify's most-streamed weekly lists in four countries, from January to August 2019, is analysed in the second part of the chapter. The chapter employs a post-humanist feminist perspective arguing that gendering is not a discursive endeavour alone, but that the media infrastructure impacts gender by design and that the algorithmic culture of Spotify is gendering popular music by making very successful artists more successful and most of these are male. Still, qualitatively analysing the artists who are most streamed also shows that the types of femininities and masculinities mostly confirm gendered and racialized stereotypes.

The last empirical chapter analyses the gender equality work performed by Keychange (www.keychange.eu). Keychange is a project initiated by the PRS Foundation in the UK and led together with Musikcentrum Öst in Sweden and Reeperbahn Festival in Germany. In 2017, Keychange presented the goal to reach 50:50 gender equality in the music industries by 2022, a goal that garnered much media attention for the project. The aim of Keychange has since changed and Keychange now provides a career programme and network for artists and innovators (women and gender minorities), a pledge for gender equality that organizations in music can join and a manifesto for policy change in the music industry, lobbied by Keychange in the European Parliament. Expressions used by Keychange, like 50:50 and gender minorities, are discussed in the chapter that also takes a closer look at how Keychange formulates the solutions for and the problems of gender inequality. These are analysed in the form they are presented online on the Keychange, PRS Foundation, Musikcentrum Öst and Reeperbahn Festival websites. Discussions about Keychange's aims, methods and participants are framed by previous research on gender equality work in the music industries. Feminist policy analysis focusing on how the solutions presented by Keychange are constructing the problems in need of solving is employed and critiques of gender mainstreaming are used as a framework to understand the strengths and weaknesses of Keychange. In the conclusion, the multiple strategies, and the networking aims in particular, are seen as strengths and reasons why this project has more potential than previous gender equality work in the music industries.

Finally, in the conclusion to this book the discussion revolves around the feminisms articulated in the examples of mediated popular music in the 2010s presented by the four case studies. The influences of intersectional feminist thought and (integrating) gender equality feminism based on a liberal understanding of the world are discussed. Further, the chapter presents gendered expressions by artists in their music, persona and lyrics that are made possible by these feminisms as expressed in popular music, how they are embedded in and affected by media development and their potential for political and structural change. Finally, the omission of an analysis on capitalism or the employment of a class perspective in the intersectional formulations of feminism in popular music is discussed. The role of capitalism in popular music is present both in the contemporary neoliberal marketization of popular music and through the historical embedment of the entertainment industry in business relying on colonialism, cheap labour in different parts of the world, war and conflict to make money. In order to challenge gender equality in popular music, feminist ideas would be strengthened by analysing the role of capitalism in popular music together with sexism, racism and trans- and homophobia.

1

Mediating the feminist superstar

Beyoncé, Lady Gaga and Taylor Swift in Netflix documentaries

In the 2010s, popular music artists addressed feminism and social justice issues in performances, speeches and social media posts in a manner not seen before. While social justice issues in music, musical performances in activism and politically engaged popular music artists have always existed, the 2010s made feminist opinions trendy in mainstream mediated popular culture. Social media and streaming services provided multiple new sites for artists to express their points of view without their opinions being filtered by journalists or the popular press. Feminism, anti-racism, lesbian, gay, bisexual, transgender, queer and others (LGBTQ+) rights and environmental politics entered the mainstream of popular music and became unsurprising themes rather than presented in isolated 'political' songs or at fund-raising galas. On her international tour *Mrs Carter* (2014), Beyoncé performed 'Flawless' in front of a sign that spelled out the word FEMINIST. The song opened with the words of author Chimamanda Ngozi Adichie reading a definition of what a feminist is (feminist: a person who believes in the social, political and economic equality of the sexes). During the Women in Music Awards in 2019, Taylor Swift delivered what was labelled 'a feminist speech' about being a woman in music. Lady Gaga spoke frankly about sexual assault and sexual harassment in the music industries in 2014 (in relation to Kesha suing Dr Luke as mentioned in the introduction of this book) and has repeatedly called herself a feminist in interviews. Being a feminist and saying so in lyrics, social media output and performances, it seems, is no longer the preserve of underground rock bands, tainted with connotations of lesbianism, cats, eccentric behaviour and (unbecoming) anger. Being a feminist and a 'slayin'' pop superstar is now compatible for women in popular music, and the artists discussed in this chapter are successful artists despite, or because of, acknowledging misogyny, racism, homophobia and discrimination. In addition to her feminist statements, Beyoncé has taken a stand for Black Lives Matter, anti-racism and the value of African-American culture. Lady Gaga's vocal support for LGBTQ+ rights, and her coming out as bisexual, has inspired scholars to coin the term 'gaga feminism' (Halberstam 2012), and while Taylor Swift was silent about politics for a long time, during the Trump presidency, she went public in support of the Democratic Party, while advocating equal rights for women and LGBTQ+ people.[1]

In this first empirical chapter of the book, I investigate the mediated feminist superstar in popular music during the 2010s. Beyoncé, Lady Gaga and Taylor Swift serve as examples, chosen for their worldwide reach and appeal. The construction of the feminist superstar in the late 2010s is examined here through examples where discursive and material articulations of feminism and gender are addressed as expressed in documentaries. The material consists of three Netflix-released music documentaries about three significant artists of the period: Lady Gaga's *Gaga: Five Foot Two* (2017) directed by Chris Moukarbels; Beyoncé's *Homecoming* (2019) directed by Beyoncé and Ed Burke; and Taylor Swift's *Miss Americana* (2020) directed by Lana Wilson. The genre of music documentaries has been claimed as a way for popular music artists to control, or at least influence, how they are represented in the media. Madonna's *Truth or dare* (1991) was an important contribution to the genre that blended the recorded concert format with backstage stories about the artist, and other performers working on Madonna's *Blond Ambition World Tour*. The concert/music documentary presents itself as a chance for listeners to get 'authentically' close to the star behind the scenes, while the artist, the chosen director or

---

[1] 'Bey feminism' has also been coined (Cooper 2016: 209) after Beyoncé. Taylor Swift's feminism has been questioned as 'fake' in the media. This chapter has the artists' feminism, seen as part of larger feminist debates, as its starting point and the theoretical perspectives used focus on feminist discourses and materializations coming through in their feminisms. Arguing that the artists are promoting completely new types of feminisms is naïve.

their team can have relative control over the narrative, unlike in tabloid stories about them. The music documentary is managed by genre rules, and like any other movie it presents an edited, selected and angled version of events. Music documentaries have grown in number and popularity following the introduction of streaming technology where production and worldwide distribution have adapted to a faster and cheaper system. Releasing a Netflix documentary is faster and cheaper than premiering it in cinemas, and has the potential to reach a larger audience too since Netflix had more than 200 million subscribers in the fourth quarter of 2020 (and viewing numbers could be even higher since one subscriber may share the subscription with a household of people).

The aim of this chapter is to investigate what feminisms the feminist superstars are representing, and what are the strengths and weaknesses of their political stances. I address this aim firstly by using theories and concepts from previous research about post-feminist popular culture and a post-feminist sensibility (Gill 2017) to understand the mediation of feminist musical stardom. The post-feminist condition in popular culture and media is defined as what happens when feminist ideas and individual women's success are taken into account (McRobbie 2009) in narratives aimed at larger audiences. Critically reading popular music feminism as a post-feminist culture entails focusing on the weaknesses of the feminist message like individualization, the lack of attention to global injustices and the 'branding' of feminism to sell things. Such interpretations, however relevant, fail to acknowledge the importance of popular music feminism for audiences, and the sincere feminist work done by artists in popular culture. Therefore, reparative readings of the artists' feminist aesthetics are also considered in this chapter. Reparative readings focus on the positive affects (Sedgwick 2003), like affinity and hope, and their potential for political upheaval. In this chapter, I find such affinity and hope in focusing on how affective solidarity with audiences and groups is central to the artists' feminist performances.[2] I argue that the artists' connections with their audiences in the documentaries are highly affective. The moments when

---

[2] Methodologically, the chapter builds on close readings of the documentaries using post-feminist and reparative theoretical perspectives for selecting key scenes to discuss.

they affectively touch their audiences with feminist messages make room for another way of understanding contemporary feminist stardom (not as post-feminist) through affect. In the conclusion of the chapter, the significance of streaming technology and social media for feminist artists' success in popular music in the 2010s is discussed in relation to the streaming service that has released all three documentaries: Netflix.

Feminism, post-feminism and popular music

Defining feminism is not a straightforward endeavour. While many ideas about feminism and feminists circulate in culture and society, there are also many kinds of feminists and feminisms. An encyclopaedic definition of feminism is the political struggle for women to have the same rights as men in society. This definition is also similar to Adichie's, as used by Beyoncé: men and women are equal. These definitions make it easy to understand why there have been feminist struggles for the right to vote, the right to equal pay for equal work, to receive an education, to get access to childcare and reproductive rights. bell hooks (1984) has defined feminism as the struggle against any kind of sexist oppression and exploitation, and as a struggle that does not ignore other forms of oppression (class oppression, racial and ethnic oppression, etc.). Turning the problem around and moving from a discourse of rights for a defined group to the combatting of power through sexist oppression has the advantage of including more subtle ways that women, including transwomen and other oppressed genders, are treated as inferior because of their gender. hooks also emphasizes the importance for feminism to consider interlinkages with other forms of oppression besides sexism, for example racism, homophobia, capitalism and colonialism. The tendency in feminist theory to understand oppressions as interacting, and gender as interacting with other sociocultural categories, was discussed in the introduction of this book. Sexist oppression, and other oppressions, also play out in cultural representations, in the home and in the family, in the expectations of workplaces and in social encounters as well as in financial imbalances, access to political power and exposure to violence. These different areas of oppression have inspired much research and public discussion. For fifty years or more, there has been an ongoing intrafeminist debate about the subject of feminism itself, concerned with who should be included in 'woman'. If we focus on rights for predefined social groups (like 'women'), it becomes harder to see the interplay of several types of oppressions, than if we focus on oppressions playing out as constructing social groups in the process. In this chapter, and throughout this book, the political call for rights and equality will repeatedly clash with intersectional analysis of oppression and gender.

Discussions about feminism as a political practice and ideological tradition have been taking place in cultural debates and in the media for centuries, and countless books, works of art and films have investigated feminist issues and made feminist claims (e.g. Pollock 1999, Kuhn 1982, Cixous 1976). It can, however, be argued that, with some exceptions, feminism before the 1980s was a subject that influenced the avant-garde arts, political speeches and the cultures of intellectuals. In mainstream popular culture, exemplified here by popular music, feminism made appearances only in certain genres or in certain times and places. One such moment was the socially engaged music movements of the 1960s, another example is punk from the 1970s.

However, in the 1980s and 1990s, feminist issues and ideas started taking previously unseen forms in mainstream mediated popular culture (Dow 1996). Researchers especially paid attention to feminist issues and topics in film and television drama where working women made an entrance as the main protagonists, for example in the much-discussed US television programme *Cagney and Lacey* (Lodz 2001) and the film *Working Girl*. This phenomenon was labelled 'post-feminism' or 'post-feminist culture' due to scholars arguing (McRobbie 2004: 4) that popular cultural texts took feminist questions into account to show that gender equality had been achieved and, with this move, undoing the need for further feminist struggles. The post-feminist cultural texts did not address feminist politics explicitly using the word 'feminism' nor did they bring forward the huge global power and wealth imbalances affecting women (Tasker & Negra 2007: 5), rather they presented a world where women were free to choose, to work, to consume, to marry – or not. Post-feminism has been understood by feminist scholars researching culture and media in the 1990s and the 2000s as showing itself in popular culture but mirroring a larger discourse in Western society, a discourse taking feminism into account that is possible *because* of feminist struggles but that does not recognize (contemporary) the need for feminist struggles in the West. Yvonne Tasker and Diane Negra (2007: 1) argue that representations of feminist issues in popular mainstream culture labelled post-feminist are coloured by the idea that feminism has passed, whether the passing of feminism is noted, mourned or celebrated. They further argue that post-feminist culture holds forth images of women who are individually successful and promotes beauty ideals, treating feminism as a commodity by selling cultural products and a lifestyle with ideals based on feminist issues. Such discourse is exemplified by Tasker and Negra (2007) with the slogan 'Girl Power'. In post-feminist culture, the protagonists are mostly white, Western and wealthy enough to 'choose' to work *and* have a family, rather than having to work as a necessity to earn money for their family (see also McRobbie 2009, Butler 2004).

Further, Tasker and Negra (2007) place post-feminist culture within a wider 'market populism' growing under neoliberalism and affecting most of the world from the 1980s onward. In market populism, market forces have incorporated former 'niche' or 'avant-garde' culture as marketable to 'niche' groups. While the word niche is misleading, women and Black people are not small groups. Market populism is the capitalist logic that identifies feminism, or anti-racism, as marketable ideas that can be used to sell stuff: from T-shirts to streams of music. As I am sure the reader has already noticed, the articulation of (post) feminism in popular culture is different in 2022 compared to the 1990s. Words like feminism, racism, misogyny and homophobia have been used in popular culture, exposing inequality. The debates around such political issues are also increasingly intermedial and occur in television dramas, social media, the news and popular music as well as during rallies and protests. Feminism and racism are spoken about in popular culture today, but what are the differences between the current mediated feminisms and the post-feminist aesthetics from twenty or thirty years ago?

Rosalind Gill (2016) argues that post-feminism is still alive when many of the feminist questions raised in the media are treated as curiosity news and quickly abandoned, making no serious impact. While 'feminism' is spoken of in the 2010s, Gill argues that post-feminism is a sensibility with changing characteristics that are indeed affective. In the 2010s, a culture of confidence, resilience and a positive attitude (performed by women) was included in post-feminist popular culture, through for example reality television, and an idea of insecurity and vulnerability as toxic (for women) was presented, such feelings were to be overcome through positive sentiments achieved by individual women (Gill 2017: 620). Examples of this post-feminist sensibility include makeover reality shows and other kinds of self-improvement television formats, focusing on improving the whole woman, not just her looks. When Gill (2017) argues that post-feminism became hegemonic in the 2010s, she shows an interest in discourse as it takes form in popular cultural texts. Her concept 'post-feminist sensibility' on the contrary involves the uses and publics, the circulation of ideas through culture, where some emotional states are deemed preferable in post-feminist culture (happiness, positivity). The later developments of theoretical discussions on post-feminism – the popularization of feminist ideas in media and culture – have given rise to new interlinked concepts: neoliberal feminism and popular feminism.[3] Catherine Rottenberg (2018) discusses the discursive dominance of neoliberal feminism in culture and media in the 2010s, arguing that feminism is present in mainstream media culture, but that the type of feminism presented is a neoliberal feminism where individual rather than collective and political solutions to feminist problems are proposed.[4] Sarah Banet-Weiser (2018) has interrogated what she labels popular feminism, a mediated feminism co-existing and battling with misogyny, moving from issue to issue often with already privileged groups as advocates. In popular feminism, making feminists claims, for example on social media, is the main output of feminism and the claims are not translated into other actions. The common denominator between research on post-feminism, neoliberal feminism and popular feminism is the critical investigation of how feminism takes place in popular media during neoliberal capitalism.

---

[3] Marketplace feminism, commodity feminism and so on have also been introduced as concepts. Post-feminism is, however, the most circulated, used and theorized concept explaining the combination of feminist ideas and market capitalism in media discourse.
[4] Neoliberalism's incorporation of feminist ideas also reaches outside of media discourse, into organizational work and political spheres for example. Here, popular culture and media discourse are in focus.

The post-feminist sensibility has been drawn upon to examine how post-feminism comes to light in popular music culture. Simone Krüger Bridge (2020) discusses how post-feminism is expressed in popular music and uses Lady Gaga and Miley Cyrus as examples of how hypersexualization, sex-positivity and individualism are used to brand female popular music artists as feminist and cool, drawing on post-feminist ideas. Kim De Laat (2019) has concluded that US love songs on the Billboard Top 100 performed by Black women artists construct an affirmative Black femininity, where the protagonist has her own money, does not tolerate infidelity and is empowered through expressions of love. Even though De Laat argues that this is a 'positive' ideal for Black femininity, she concludes that while the ideal constructed is in contrast with previous negative stereotypes of Black femininity, these stereotypes live on through their negation. Robin James (2020) has argued that popular feminism, post-feminism and neoliberal feminism influence contemporary music culture in several works. For example, in investigating expressions of resilience (James 2015) in mainstream popular music, she discusses how strength, for female artists, is presented as overcoming difficulties by oneself as an individual.[5] Her analysis fits well with the post-feminist critique of individual success stories replacing collective political struggles as a feminist method. Scholars studying Beyoncé have discussed the tension in her career between her feminism and individualism, capitalism and appropriation of, for example, African musics (Baade & McGee 2021: 7). These tensions between feminism and commodification will be discussed in this chapter in relation to all three artists.

The documentaries

The three music documentaries analysed all depict feminist superstars by combining onstage, backstage and what appears to be private footage of the

---

[5] The resilience and feminism of popular music artists have also been investigated in other times, and from other perspectives; for example, in the work of Black female blues artists in the United States (Davis 1998: 47). The dominance of post-feminist discourse in the 2010s does not mean that the ideas expressed are entirely new.

artists. The balance between the onstage and other footage differs: *Homecoming* includes most of Beyoncé's *Coachella* performance of 2017 in the order it was performed, a small amount of private footage and footage from the rehearsals for the *Coachella* show presented as an in-between place, more private than the onstage material, but still presenting the artist in a professional role. There is, for example, no footage from Beyoncé's home(s?), and only one scene where she is pictured in a private social setting, hosting a party for family and friends in a garden. *Homecoming* uses quotes from known African-American public intellectuals to frame the rehearsals and the performance. *Gaga: Five Foot Two* never depicts Lady Gaga's *Superbowl* performance that the documentary builds up to, but the first and the last footage in the documentary show her being lifted by wires to perform at the Superbowl, the performance we never see (Figure 1.1). Most of the documentary follows the artist around, the unseen production team follow her workday and interview her in informal settings. It also contains partial performances by Lady Gaga, one at the Democratic National Convention. *Gaga: Five Foot Two* has a different balance

Figure 1.1 Lady Gaga ascends for her *Superbowl* half-time performance in 2017 (Getty Images).

from *Homecoming* where the 'private' footage dominates the documentary since Lady Gaga is seen in her home, her car, her studio, with her parents, at a baptism, etc. The music recording and performances are used to frame the personal story that is told in fractions of conversations with Lady Gaga. *Miss Americana* is structured in a similar way to *Gaga: Five Foot Two* with the narrative following the artist and her music making in everyday settings. Taylor Swift's music, lyrics and performances are used to further the story – not to stand by themselves. Taylor Swift's entire career is investigated in *Miss Americana* while the interviews and private footage are from a shorter period, 2018–19. The timeline in *Miss Americana* is not fully chronological, yet the documentary narratively builds on the important events of her career from childhood to the present, with the events presented in the order that they took place. The format of *Miss Americana* is therefore more conventional than the other two documentaries, because it depicts the artist's career chronologically, and because Taylor Swift is speaking a lot as a talking head, explaining what has happened and how she felt about it, effectively narrating her own story. She talks and explains more than Lady Gaga, and much more than Beyoncé. Beyoncé is instead talking through her performance and in voice over; and in *Gaga: Five Foot Two*, the story is narrated around the recording and release of Lady Gaga's album, *Joanne*, built on both what is depicted in footage and what is said.

The three documentaries narratively construct the personalities, personal lives, struggles and successes of the three artists. In the documentaries, their ways of working with and through personal and professional problems fuel the narrative structure of the films. Another feature that the three documentaries have in common is that they build a timeline towards a performance or record release: Beyoncé is working to put together her *Coachella* performance; Lady Gaga is working on her album *Joanne* and towards her *Superbowl* show; and Taylor Swift is looking back on her career so far, while working in her studio on her album *Lover*, and performing on her *Reputation* tour. All three artists have claimed feminist positions and express feminist views in the documentaries, and while the concept of feminism is not discussed, several significant feminist issues are. The following analysis of the representations of the artists in the documentaries is structured in three sections: first the presentation of the artists' personality, personal life and struggles as shown in the documentaries is analysed; second, the presentation of the artists' way of dealing with problems and moving past them is discussed; and finally their feminist aesthetics and politics are analysed, looking in particular at affective aspects of the artists' performances, as shown in the documentaries, these are discussed in relation to the audiences engaged and the groups evoked.

Meeting the artists

All three documentaries are using the personal experiences and difficulties of the artists to build a story where success is achieved. In *Homecoming*, Beyoncé describes her twin pregnancy, which preceded the rehearsal for her *Coachella* performance, as 'extremely difficult'. She talks about how she suffered multiple complications during the pregnancy and tells the viewers that the day she gave birth to twins by emergency C-section, she was 218 pounds. This personal narrative is crucial for the structure of the documentary, which is built around the story of the work leading to the performance at *Coachella* that is also shown, piece by piece, in the documentary. Beyoncé's personal route through rehearsals to performance is only introduced after the first part of the stage performance has been shown, and the context of Historical Black Colleges and Universities (HBCU) inspiring the show has been discussed, African-American intellectuals have been quoted and Beyoncé's creative leadership over the ambitious *Coachella* performance has been established. The personal difficulties are thus not presented as the first or only context of significance, but are presented in the longest sequence of personal footage in the documentary. Here, Beyoncé's newborn babies, an ultrasound being performed on her pregnant stomach and a person being rolled in a hospital bed are shown in what appear to be home videos. The journey from starting rehearsals for the show to taking the bus to perform at *Coachella* structures the narrative of the backstage story, with the birth of the twins presented as the important starting point of this journey.

The physical and mental difficulties of returning after childbirth to perform professionally is of relevance to those who have given birth and work in the performing arts. Beyoncé says: 'there were days when I thought, [. . .] I would never be the same, physically my strength and endurance would never be the same.' Her voice is talking over images. In the documentary, she never appears as a talking head being interviewed. This aspect of the documentary hinders the audience from looking at her talking. The story is told from her perspective with her words leading the story presented in images. When she is describing the physical pain of getting her body back in shape, her storytelling is accompanied by images of her working out and rehearsing dance routines. The body and the specific toll her work as a performing artist takes on her body are discussed, and it becomes clear that dancing and singing on stage is no easy job.

> In order for me to meet my goal I am limiting myself to no bread, no carbs, no sugar, no dairy, no meat, no fish, no alcohol and, [sigh] I am hungry. Just trying to figure out how to balance being a mother of a 6-year-old and twins that need me and giving myself creatively and physically. It was a lot to juggle.

This quote highlights the physical pain of training and dieting along with the mental pain. Beyoncé talks about how hard it is to juggle work and parenthood. The work life–family life axis, as has been discussed in feminism, in the life of a popular music performer is inscribed on the material body itself. Ideals of motherhood, 'a 6-year-old and twins that need me', and ideals of a superstar performer's body seem to take a toll not only physically but also mentally and emotionally. Being away from her children for long hours of work during the eight-month period of rehearsing for the show is described as difficult. 'My mind was not there, my mind wanted to be with my children, what people don't see is the sacrifice', she says. Scholars investigating post-feminism in popular culture have discussed how, in representations of women, having a career and having a family have been narrated as a contradiction and a 'problem to juggle' for women in post-feminist popular culture. In early scholarly discussions about post-feminist discourse, Rachel Moseley and Jacinda Read (2002) argue that the 1990s television show *Ally McBeal* was concerned with negotiating combinations of a professional career and personal happiness for women, a key topic for post-feminist popular culture then and now. In the show, the distinction between the public and the private is blurred (Moseley & Read 2002: 245), for example by Ally using her private experiences to succeed in her career. According to Moseley and Read (2002: 247), *Ally McBeal* demonstrates the difficulty of wanting a career and a family, representing femininity and feminism, appealing to an audience of white, middle-class women struggling with the same desires. The show presents no clear solution to these problems. The tension between family and work, or the private and the public, is clearly presenting itself as a difficulty for Beyoncé 'juggling' her children and her *Coachella* rehearsals. The documentary does not detail how she manages to work through this dilemma, but she does say that she had never challenged herself this much before and that it was hard, implying that she got through it by hard work since the hardship was described as in the past.

According to Catherine Rottenberg (2014: 433), individual performance, individuation and happiness as tools have been presented as solutions to the problem of family–work balance for successful women in what she labels neoliberal feminist discourse. The individuated neoliberal feminist subject (Rottenberg 2014: 420) is aware of the inequalities between men and women, but accepts responsibility for her own well-being and self-care in professional success, turning inequality into an individual problem that she can solve by 'leaning in'. Gender inequality in relation to family responsibilities is not addressed head-on in *Homecoming*. Beyoncé is represented as the head of her family; she occupies the director's chair during rehearsals, her (very famous) husband sits beside her or stands in the back and he brings the children to rehearsals. Her family is presented as revolving around her, but they also need her, especially the children and therefore she is responsible for her family, as a mother. This is never questioned and solving the work life–family life balance is not presented as a question for anyone but herself, rendering structural solutions invisible. Without diminishing Beyoncé's personal difficulties, there are many parallels to the discourse analysed by Rottenberg (2014) in the sense that the problems presented are physical, emotional and mental, not practical or financial. The twins need breastfeeding, but the cost of childcare, the need to feed her family and put a roof over their head are not discussed as a problem. Beyoncé's problem with parenting as presented in the documentary is mostly emotional and mental. The children need their mother as a present figure in their lives and her work as a superstar artist does not allow her to focus on them during rehearsals.

Lady Gaga and Taylor Swift are both about thirty years old in their respective documentaries and have neither children nor husbands. They indicate that they may want a partner/boyfriend in their lives. In some parts of the documentaries, they talk about boyfriends they do have, but the boyfriends are not central to the storylines. Taylor Swift mentions that she is not ready to 'have kids', but in saying that she is opening up to being ready in the future. *Gaga: Five Foot Two* starts off with a scene depicting Lady Gaga in her home in Malibu, California. Dressed in casual clothes, she feeds her dogs, jokes around with friends, family and staff in the kitchen (they are not introduced to the viewers and it is therefore unclear if they are friends, family or staff) and proceeds to go upstairs for a massage. During this scene, she discloses that she is arguing with her boyfriend, she is done with taking 'bullshit' from men and she is feeling sexier than ever at thirty. While she walks upstairs, she explains why her house is full of balloons: because she has just signed a movie contract to play the lead role in *A Star Is Born*. While there are other people in her house, they are not presented as significant others. Later in the documentary, her parents and grandmother are introduced as the closest family the viewers get to meet. The opening scene establishes Lady Gaga as independent, with her own home, dogs, staff and career. She does not live with a partner, children, parents or other family members. Angela McRobbie (2007) outlines what she calls a new sexual contract for white, Western, middle-class women, where participation in consumer culture, sexual freedom and control over one's reproduction together with a successful career is depicted as the new ideal way of being a woman. This ideal, argues McRobbie (2007: 733), is creating a consumer citizenship branded as freedom and choice for young (heterosexual) women.[6] The young, free, successful woman is reinvented, argues McRobbie, she is imagined as in control, and becomes a new ideal that results in a backlash for young women failing to meet these standards, by, for example,

---

[6] The heterosexuality of the sexual contract may be more inclusive in 2022, where LGBTQ+ rights are more spoken about and more included in popular culture in shows like *The Bold Type*.

falling pregnant or failing in school (McRobbie 2007: 731), not following beauty standards or failing at careers. Often, such 'failing' young women are over-represented in poor, Black, brown and immigrant communities. Lady Gaga is successful in her career, she is feeling sexy and confident, and she is not dependent on a man (yet she has access to one). Her heterosexuality has not been presented as stable in her career, she has described herself as bisexual, later as heterosexual and is known to date men.[7] The core features of her artist persona are established in the first scene of the documentary and sit well with McRobbie's description of a 'top girl' successful in her career, heterosexual (enough), white, free, confident and affluent. One thing that diverts from McRobbie's characterization of the new sexual contract is that there is no need for Lady Gaga to denounce feminism, in the way McRobbie observed in the early 2000s, she has embraced it. The popularity of feminism in celebrity culture in the 2010s has been analysed by Sarah Banet-Weiser (2018: 4) who argues that popular feminism is affirmative, cheering on activities like gender equality marches, hash tags and go-get-them attitudes for women. Popular feminism rarely addresses the details of the difficult structural problems behind the slogans, or economic, global and racial disparities in contemporary society. This chapter will not argue that Lady Gaga is simply a popular feminist, as you will see later, but it is reasonable to problematize the way she capitalizes on her politics without too much risk involved as a sexually free, career-minded, beautiful and beautified white woman at thirty. In the documentary, Lady Gaga's top girl persona is complicated by her 'demons', something historically associated with male geniuses in the arts. We are told about her physical and mental health problems: her chronic hip pain and her panic attacks. Further on in the documentary, she talks about loneliness in relation to not having a partner after breaking up with her boyfriend. Her success and independence are therefore presented as having a downside: bad health and loneliness. Lady Gaga reflects on being touched and surrounded by people all day and contrasts

---

[7] Lady Gaga's sex life is not in focus here, rather the analysis understands her presentation of herself in the documentary as mostly heterosexual – she talks only about boyfriends as love and sex interests – but not entirely heterosexual because of previous statements. Lady Gaga's self-identity and practiced sexuality is out of reach for the viewer.

it with being so alone in the evening when they all leave. Her top girl persona is independent but lonely. In a similar vein, Taylor Swift asks 'shouldn't I have someone I could call right now?' when she describes the loneliness she felt after winning multiple awards for her album *1989* and achieving many of her (previous) professional goals. Being a successful female artist, in her story too, is described as lonely.

A key scene for the narrative of *Miss Americana* is when Taylor Swift describes the impact on her of the scandal at the 2009 MTV Video Music Awards. This was when Kanye West interrupted her speech to tell the audience that she did not deserve to win the award she was holding. Another key scene is when she describes the 2016 social media hate campaign targeting her. Both incidents impacted on her mental health she says, and in 2016 she went into hiding (from the public) for a year. Falling out of grace in the media and with fans, and hearing booing at the MTV Video Music Awards are described as having had a profound effect on her. 'I had to deconstruct an entire belief system' she states, and this quote is also used in the trailer for the documentary. The narrative of Taylor Swift being a 'good girl' in need of waking up to a complicated an unequal reality is presented from the beginning of the documentary. These incidents are her wake-up calls.

In the opening scene of the film, Taylor Swift plays the piano, pets a kitten and reads her first diary, 'the main thing that I always tried to be was . . . just a good girl', Taylor Swift says. She is positioning herself as always having wanted to be good at what she did, and for people to like and admire her. She says 'a nice girl smiles and waves and says thank you, a nice girl doesn't make people feel uncomfortable with her views'. Taylor Swift is going back in time after positioning us in the present by reading her diary in the 'now', and this is illustrated with footage of her as a young and smiling performer. After establishing the timeline of her career between 2002 and 2016, the documentary focuses on her year of change. She says, 'when people decided I was . . . wicked and evil and conniving and not a good person that was the one that I couldn't really bounce back [from].' The documentary depicts her writing for the album *Lover*: being both lonely and starting a new romantic relationship. This relationship is not in focus in the documentary. Rather, the change in Taylor Swift is described as her moving from being an artist who strives to be 'good' to becoming a new improved person who can be open with her views and her personality. The new Taylor Swift has deconstructed her belief system, she answers back and speaks about politics, mental health and sexual abuse. The second half of the documentary focuses on this Taylor Swift and the later years of her career. Even though Taylor Swift has been speaking up for women's rights, and for herself, since before 2016, it is the time after her seclusion that is presented as her political time in *Miss Americana*.

The makeover paradigm, where women are supposed to better themselves in how they dress, think, work, look after their children and clean their houses, is, according to Gill (2017), central in post-feminist popular culture. Jessica Ringrose and Valerie Walkerdine (2008) have argued that the 'reinvention' process is inclined to strive towards a betterment that mirrors respectable middle-class femininity, where the working-class woman is presented as abject. They have analysed makeover reality television where, they argue, the working-class woman does not become a subject until she is 'made over'. Around the same time as the election of Donald Trump, Taylor Swift's 'good' middle-class femininity fell out of favour in the media and was labelled as 'fake', a label put on her during the social media hate campaign in 2016. This happened after her persona had been very popular during an (already) long career. Taylor Swift's reinvention of her image did not happen overnight, it can be seen in lyrics, videos and social media posts. In *Miss Americana*, the change is simplified for the narrative structure. It is presented as her going into hiding to write *Reputation*, after the scorn and hate she received, then she returns a better person and now she is successful again. In the now, she is performing on the *Reputation* tour and writing *Lover*, and by the end of the film she has finished these two endeavours. The improvement she made is presented as mental improvement; as discussed by Gill (2017), she reached the right state of mind. Affective positivity and mental strength are presented as goals and solutions in post-feminist culture. In the documentary, other aspects of Taylor Swift's pre-awakening personality are presented and discussed; 'we do not do that anymore' she says repeatedly, referring to almost being triggered by looking fat in a photo. Taylor Swift discusses the eating disorders that she has overcome, and images of her younger and skinnier self are shown to accompany the story. In the documentary, the new and stronger Taylor Swift builds neatly on a successful individual narrative of overcoming difficulties by improving her mind and body (she eats now).

The consequences of her improvement were not only individual, but Taylor Swift also became engaged in political lobbying and politically organized activism after 2016, as presented in the documentary. Reinvention is thematized in *Gaga: Five Foot Two* when Lady Gaga repeatedly returns to how the album she is recording, *Joanne*, will show a more personal Lady Gaga and a different more honest side to her. Not just the personal topics of the lyrics but also her clothes, make-up and music are subject to change in the documentary. In a post-feminist analysis of reinvention, the process of the artists transforming themselves is neither true nor false but displays the individualization and marketization of women and feminism in the twenty-first century. Ironically, there is a scene in *Miss Americana* where Taylor Swift speaks critically of the need for female artists to reinvent themselves to stay new and interesting. She argues that this is not necessary in the same way for male artists and that her expiry date might be up soon, pointing to inequalities between male and female artists' career paths over time. While she is performing the post-feminist logic of makeover, the documentary is acknowledging the makeover paradigm and critiquing it. Being conscious of rebranding does not stop Taylor Swift from releasing *Miss Americana*, a rebranding and rewriting of herself.

Achieving and moving on

In a scene in *Homecoming* shown after the presentation of her experienced hardship with getting fit and rehearsing after pregnancy and delivery, Beyoncé fits into a stage costume. She appears very excited, smiling and laughing, and her assistant (or friend, the person is not introduced to the viewers) calls her husband who does not seem to understand the importance of Beyoncé's slimmer figure fitting the costume. When they hang up, the person who was calling him for Beyoncé comments that men just don't understand. For Beyoncé, dieting and working out are presented in the documentary as a path to getting back, from being pregnant, from having a C-section, from not performing. When she fits into the costume, it is a symbolic moment of success that men can't understand; the documentary is rendering the success as a feminine experience. She was able to get back in shape, she succeeded. Simultaneously, it shows Beyoncé seeking to share her success with her husband, without him understanding its importance. Gill (2017: 617) argues that self-monitoring and self-optimization are cornerstones of a post-feminist sensibility where the social media landscape and the increased use of apps for beauty and visual social media activity require the female body to be beautiful. According to Gill (2017: 607), this evolving paradigm controlled by the individuals being monitored (by themselves and others) is a site where both the body and one's internal life are up for improvement and editing. Thus, improvement for women in post-feminist media culture is not only physical, achieving your dream body, but also mental, using self-help techniques to improve your performance at work or to learn to love yourself. Beyoncé's improvement is here presented as physical, unlike Taylor Swift's rebuilding of herself as a person. Social media is one place where self-optimization takes on a concrete shape, through the filtering and editing of selfies. There is a scene in *Miss Americana* concerned with fitting into costumes where Taylor Swift just about fits into a dress, but cannot move freely in it, before going on stage. In her documentary, Lady Gaga records a music video in boots that make her feet bleed and she comments that she did not want to stop because the filming was going so well. Her hip pain, featured as one theme throughout the documentary, was caused by a broken hip during the *Born this way* tour, attributed to the toll of the performances on the tour instead of a single incident. Changing the clothes, boots or choreographies to fit their bodies is not presented as an option in either of these scenes in the documentaries.

Neoliberalism's core ideals of choice, individuality and self-determination are central in post-feminist culture. To look inwards (Gill 2017: 610–11), improving one's personality and even one's emotions, is highlighted in post-feminist discourse, as has been discussed. Nevertheless, it is also important to achieve success and to look good. As seen in the examples above, 'choice' may be thought of as infinite but is rather limited. Feminist superstars may have a choice in what body, clothes or shoes they perform in, but the choice is limited by beauty standards that (in the documentaries) hurt them. Their self-determination to push through mental, emotional and physical pain is what helps them achieve success. A common denominator for self-improvement in post-feminist culture is that the individual is responsible for her own betterment. Post-feminist cultural products like self-help books, advisers and make-up artists can help her, and the result of the betterment is presented as positive and an achievement, not as a repressive culture where women must change their bodies and minds to fit in. Angela McRobbie (2007: 626) addressed this move in post-feminist culture when observing that the dominance of voluntaristic beauty regimes masks the patriarchal order as 'choice' while beauty standards are intact. When Beyoncé works hard, by her own choice, to get her body back and, at the same time, embarks on a mental and intellectual journey to perform the HBCU cultural legacy at *Coachella*. This narrative of *Homecoming* fits neatly into a post-feminist cultural pattern. Nobody requires this of her. Beyoncé herself laughs and says: 'I definitely pushed myself further than I knew I could, and I learned a very valuable lesson. I will never [laughing] push myself that far again.' While acknowledging that she took on too much, her laughter is happy and she displays pride in her achievement. The performance is constructed as the main achievement and fitting into her costume is narrated as an important step on the road to the *Coachella* stage, as are auditions of dancers, music rehearsals, dance rehearsals, costume designs and planning. All these elements are shown as hard work in *Homecoming*. The large group of performers, musicians and backstage workers involved is emphasized as important in the documentary, as is their (Black US) diversity. Beyoncé is presented as the mastermind behind the performance, seated in the director's chair, and there are no interviews with sound producers, managers, her husband or other family members to question her individual artistic control over the show. The collective process of the performers she recruits and Beyoncé's leadership are not contradictory. A collective process to celebrate southern Black culture is presented *as* her vision. The show is not only a collaboration with many, but also all about Beyoncé.

In the final scenes of *Miss Americana*, Taylor Swift is talking about how liberating it has been for her to speak out politically, becoming an activist working with the 'Violence Against Women Act' and the 'Equality Act'. She is shown recording the video for 'You Need to Calm Down' with a group of LGBTQ+ friends and collaborators. She looks happy and is interacting with friends. The documentary narrates her mental journey of self-discovery and self-improvement that has changed her from being a 'pleaser', a girl waiting to be admired, to a woman working for what she thinks is important. Central to post-feminist discourse is that the individual is not 'stuck' in traditional gendered social and cultural patterns but surpasses them (McRobbie 2007), a subject that exists 'after' feminism. Taylor Swift names her sexual assault trial as an(other) awakening on her journey from a 'good girl'. In her story, the term 'feminism' is not mentioned, but her growth is into a political woman – the social groups she advocates for are working for women and LGBTQ+ people (Figure 1.2). Beyoncé, on the other hand, is presenting her tribute to Black southern culture in the United States, in all its forms, bodies and expressions. Black southern US culture is the political and aesthetic message of the performance and the documentary. Beyoncé is the first Black woman to headline *Coachella* – this is given significance in the documentary and she wants to own it. After her performance, *Coachella* should be renamed 'Beychella', referring to her nickname 'Bey'. By including Black southern culture influences in the dance,

Figure 1.2 Taylor Swift receives a Video of the Year Award for 'You Need to Calm Down' with some of the cast from the video at the MTV Video Music Awards in 2019 (Getty Images).

dancers, band, cheerleaders, intellectuals and costumes, Beyoncé is also, in effect, allowing a Black southern audience to own *Coachella*, a mainstream popular music festival that is celebrated by the (white) avant-garde and located in California. Her move is a denunciation of the white dominance of popular music festivals, the male dominance and the coastal (East/West) dominance of US popular music. The documentary's existence is ensuring that the audience will not forget her performance.

Lady Gaga speaks frankly about her difficulties while growing up in the music industries, arguing that it is hard to become famous at a young age and to change in the celebrity circuit. In *Gaga: Five Foot Two*, Lady Gaga is narrating a story about growing up at thirty by recording and promoting the album *Joanne*, named after her father's sister who died at a young age. The album, she states, is different from her previous albums by being more personal and less oriented towards the disco-pop genre that made her famous. She is also working with different people. Most importantly, Lady Gaga is presenting her producer Mark Ronson as different from all the other male producers with whom she has worked. She is implying that some of her previous producers tried to control her, sexualize her and make her feel like she needed them to have value as a pop star. While Lady Gaga's story of growing up in the music industries is not as pedagogically narrated as Taylor Swift's story – for example, no sections in *Gaga: Five Foot Two* look back at Lady Gaga's previous career moments – she is striving forward with her most personal album so far, wanting to be more honest. And she had also landed the lead in *A Star Is Born*, a movie that changed her image after the filming of the documentary. The third feminist superstar, Beyoncé, is not presented as needing to grow up. She is married and the mother of three children. Her performances in *Homecoming* celebrate a twenty-year-long career. Her growing up has passed in a heteronormative timeline, and she has arrived but not without sacrifice.

Feminism, southern Black culture and LGBTQ+ rights

Thus far, the analysis has used the framework of post-feminist culture and post-feminist sensibility to understand the documentaries. While watching them and considering the importance of feminist superstars to audiences, I strongly felt that it was not enough to understand what type of feminism is represented, but to understand how it touches audiences and what it does affectively. Beyoncé's performance of 'Don't Hurt Yourself' during *Homecoming* includes a quote from Malcom X: 'The most disrespected person in America is the black woman. The most unprotected person in America is the black woman. The most neglected person in America is the black woman.' This quote, from 1962, connects racism and sexism in an additive argument. Malcom X's critique of structural racism in the United States is, in this quote, heightened by Black women's situation, since the Black woman faces racism and sexism (Figure 1.3). While Black feminist scholars have complicated the intersections of race and gender in the United States, most famously Kimberlé Crenshaw (1991), which are also being produced by class divisions, the quote still effectively articulates an affinity between racism and sexism. Beyoncé's *Coachella* performance is

Figure 1.3 Beyoncé performs 'Crazy in Love' with a large brass band at the Coachella Valley Music and Arts Festival in 2018 (Getty Images).

embedded in Black feminist ideas by using quotes from famous Black feminists in the documentary: Alice Walker, Toni Morrison and Maya Angelou among others. Black feminists are also known to speak out about the ramifications of economic inequalities for Black US women. In the performance, the quote by Malcom X is ambiguous, the song's lyrics and the vocal, musical and bodily expressions of the song on stage emphasize strength. Beyoncé is referring to herself as 'no average bitch' in the first verse, the rock-flavoured guitar sound of the song is accompanied by Beyoncé's headbanging and her distorted voice. The final line of the lyrics is 'you gon' lose your wife'. The song is understood by audiences and music critics as an expression of her rage after acts of infidelity within her marriage. The rage is multimodally expressed in the performance of 'Don't Hurt Yourself' at *Coachella* and the Malcom X quote inserted towards the end of the song represents the causes for this rage – being angry after being disrespected should therefore be understood as part of a reaction to systematic disrespect acted out on Black women in the United States. In 'Don't Hurt Yourself', Beyoncé is acting out violent emotions and strength as Black female resistance. But she is not doing this alone. Throughout her performance at *Coachella*, she repeatedly calls on the 'queens', 'ladies' and 'divas' in the audience, clearly feminizing the audience and involving them in the articulation of the performance. That Beyoncé's Black feminism affects her audiences inside and outside the United States is apparent (Baade & McGee 2021). While the signifiers used leave room for more than cis female identification, and it is not only cis women who are seen singing along in the crowd, it brings forward femininity associated with Blackness by the performers on stage, the framing of the show in Black culture and the style of aesthetic 'swag' that Beyoncé embodies in her vocal and physical performance. The affinity created on an emotional level, where the audience is crying, screaming and singing along to these calls, brings on an affective feminist audience. The relation of the audience to the performance is hard to grasp in just the songs, the performance and film from the backstage area. The faces of the audience watching Beyoncé, singing along, laughing and crying, are shown in the documentary, and the audience is notably touched by her performance.

The call for 'queens', 'ladies' and 'divas' could be attributed to post-feminist culture where 'girl power' and other slogans are invoked – without more than slogans. The inherent critique of the 'taken into account-ness' of feminism in capitalist popular culture seems to indicate that post-feminism is flawed, it is not real feminism. If any celebrity tries to better herself, it can be read as neoliberal rebranding – one might ask what actions are not branding within the post-feminist sensibility? Post-feminism therefore risks becoming a totalizing theory. In effect, the post-feminist critique could be extended to all culture that makes a profit (and a girl's gotta live), understanding no commercial culture as existing outside of post-feminism. In addition to not taking audience experiences and interpretations into account there is also a potential elitism in the post-feminist critique where only art that does not aim to sell can be truly feminist. Any post-feminist critique will thus fail to recognize feminist affective messages of solidarity performed by commercially successful artists.

What then would be the analytical option to use in understanding Beyoncé's performance through the affect seen on the faces of the audience? Reparative readings have been suggested to shift the focus from suspicion and paranoia in critical analysis (Sedgwick 2003: 125). Eve Kosovsky Sedgwick argued that positive affects, read as such, of cultures' attachments to ideas, other texts and artwork are in focus in a reparative reading. She (2003: 149) exemplifies with camp aesthetics and argues that in a paranoid reading they are understood as parody and a critique of the heteronormative culture while a reparative reading can see camp as a performance of love and a celebration of mainstream culture. The reparative reading was developed using Silvan Tomkins' theories of affect, where the bodily experiences of emotions are central. This, according to Sedgwick, is part of an epistemological stance, viewing knowledge as affective and performative. What we know also creates, and paranoid readings create paranoid worlds. From this perspective, post-feminist readings of feminist superstars may create paranoia, a mistrust in their feminism and anything they say or do. Rita Felski (2015) has followed Sedgwick's invitation to propose a postcritique, resisting the critical imperative of critical theory. Felski (2015: 4) argues that hope and affinity co-exist with critical caveats and proceeds to develop her version of a postcritique that allows for affirmation in interpretation. Viewing the documentaries from the perspective of a postcritique, feminism is not only appropriated but it is also acted out aesthetically in the documentaries and in other works to which they are referring. In *Homecoming*, Beyoncé places her performance in the tradition of Toni Morrison and Alice Walker, influential feminists working to combat the intersection of US racism and sexism. While Lady Gaga's most spectacular performances, for example 'Paparazzi' at the MTV Video Music Awards, are not shown in *Gaga: Five Foot Two*, they are discussed and Lady Gaga reflects on what fame does to women affectively and how she tries to enact that in her work. When Taylor Swift films 'You Need to Calm Down' with LGBTQ+ celebrities and activists – as shown in *Miss Americana* – she is acting out queer camp aesthetics and her affective affinity to queer critiques is shaped by *form* and content.

Using feminist affect theory, Clare Hemmings (2012) has argued that affective solidarity is exercised through extending the experiences of negative affect caused by sexism, racism, class, sexuality, gender identity, etc., to understand and solidarize with subjects and groups other than one's own. Exercising affective solidarity is a bodily experience with the audience and performers of popular music who can bring audiences with different experiences of, for example, sexism, racism and homophobia together as 'queens'. When Beyoncé's performance inverts the disrespect and negative affects previously connoted by Black femininity to queen-dom, affinity is created. An affective affinity has the potential to translate into political action and structural change according to Hemmings (2012).

Affective solidarity can be used to bridge differences in feminist politics over time, space and oppressions. In an early scene in *Gaga: Five Foot Two*, Lady Gaga is sitting down seemingly intoxicated, smoking a cigarette and talking to an unnamed person about music producers. She argues that male producers (Mark Ronson whom she is currently working with on the album *Joanne* excluded) get all the girls, 'the most beautiful girls', and that she has had to face and contest the sexism of the music industries where women are goods that men get. She says that when she has been asked to be sexy and pop, she 'always put a twist on it to control it'. She provides a few examples such as the meat dress, or when she performed 'Paparazzi' at the 2009 MTV Video Music Awards and ended her performance by bleeding out and dying in a peroxide blonde hairstyle and white costume. She argues in the documentary that this performance was made to honour the women hurt or killed by their fame: 'Marilyn Monroe/Norma Jean, Anna Nicole Smith, and you know who'.[8] In the performance, Lady Gaga is clearly affected at the end, while dying, and so is the audience when she starts to bleed on stage. Her affinity with other women is affectively touching the audience, potentially changing them while evoking social groups and oppressions. The presentation of this performance in the documentary is linked to the sexism she herself experienced in the music industries. Her enacting of sexism as murder is crossing time when constructing a critique of the sexism of the broad entertainment industries. Lady Gaga enacts not only affect through her murder on stage, but also affective connections with the audience choked and moved by the performance. The performance activates a lineage of white cis women. Still, an affinity with other groups has been central to Lady Gaga's career and her artistic implementation of affective solidarity. 'Born This Way' became an anthem of social justice, to feel, dance and cry with in the 2010s, in which she artistically and lyrically addresses racism, class and LGBTQ+ rights as the figure of 'mother monster'. Her alter ego poses as an outsider, a monster, and invites all who feel affinity with the outside position and oppression to be her children.

For Taylor Swift, a political awakening in US party politics is presented as an important factor in her affectively solidarizing with survivors of sexual violence and LGBTQ+ activists in *Miss Americana*. Party politics is also represented in the other two documentaries. Lady Gaga performs at the Democratic National Convention in *Gaga: Five Foot Two*; Beyoncé says, in support of Hilary Clinton, that she wants her daughter to see a female president. Taylor Swift comes out as a Democrat during the midterm elections in 2018. Her political 'coming out' on social media is narratively told together with the story of her sexual assault trial. In 2017, she won a case against a former DJ who had put his hand up her skirt and touched her behind. While Beyoncé and Lady Gaga's Democratic allegiances are minor scenes in their documentaries

---

[8] Lady Gaga does not say so, but it seems fair to assume she is referring to Madonna, with whom she has been said to have a feud, given the peroxide blond historic lineage she is enacting.

as they are well-known Democrats, Taylor Swift had previously constructed herself as an artist who did not comment on politics, and many had thought her to be a Republican because she emerged as a country artist and did not speak up. When she posted on social media her support for the Democratic candidate in the 2018 midterm elections in her home state of Tennessee, it became major news and provoked President Trump to comment that he liked her music less after knowing she was a Democrat; his commentary is included in the documentary. Narratively, her Democratic stance and her win in the sexual assault trial in *Miss Americana* lead to an emotional performance during a concert when she states that she believes in all victims of sexual violence, and to the recording of the music video for 'You Need to Calm Down' with LGBTQ+ celebrities and activists. The first example is taken from a live performance in Tampa and sees Taylor Swift emotionally moved, her voice breaking as she talks while sitting and playing at her piano on stage. She tells the audience about her assault and the trial, and finishes by saying 'I'm sorry to anyone who wasn't believed' and moves on to sing 'Clean'. The audience is huge and respond to her talking with sounds that make the aesthetic and political performance more than a statement, an affective connection is made with the audience, they respond, be they survivors of sexual assault or not. Taylor Swift also connects her distaste for Republican politics in Tennessee with her support for survivors of sexual violence when she talks about the Republican candidate who has been speaking out against the 'Violence Against Women Act', and is against gay marriage. In reaching out to (fellow) survivors of sexual violence and LGBTQ+ people, Taylor Swift is presented as taking part in formalized institutional political work. Her affective solidarity translates into organized activism. She is crying when the Democratic candidate in Tennessee loses and is glowing with happiness when the 'Equality Act' receives enough signatures to go to Parliament. The affects shown by all three artists in the documentaries are in solidarity with others and these affects are entangled with their political engagement with the Democratic Party, Black Lives Matter and LGBTQ+ rights groups. Their affective solidarity also reaches beyond slogans, when it affectively touches their audiences and translates into political structural work performed by them.

Conclusion

The artist documentaries analysed in this first chapter can be understood differently depending on if they are seen within a post-feminist framework or through reparative readings. They are embedded in contemporary media, the documentaries disseminated on the streaming service Netflix. Netflix is the largest streaming service for film and television in the world with more than 200 million paying subscribers in 2021 and the three documentaries are all Netflix released. I have argued at length for affective connections with audiences opening for feminist, anti-racist and LGBTQ+ friendly politics. The audiences discussed so far have been the live audiences shown in the documentaries. What happens to reparative readings and translations of such into political action when the Netflix audience sees the documentaries? Netflix orders and promotes content, like music documentaries, to some users more than others. This may lead to audiences interested in music, feminism and female artists being recommended to watch these documentaries and being affected by their messages of feminism, anti-racism and LGBTQ+ rights. Audiences outside of those already interested in the issues may also watch and be affectively touched by them, moved to become engaged in feminist politics.

The aim of this chapter was to investigate what feminisms the feminist superstars are representing, and what are the strengths and weaknesses of their political stances. It is very possible to argue that a post-feminist sensibility frames the three artists in their Netflix-released documentaries by promoting success stories of individual women, balancing work–family life, a makeover paradigm and the importance of positive emotions and mental improvement as they reinvent themselves. Without the divided capitalist market to sell female, Black, LGBTQ+ and feminist goods, there would be no documentaries about the struggles of Beyoncé, Lady Gaga and Taylor Swift. Still, as I have argued, the analytical framework drawn from scholarly work concerned with a post-feminist sensibility in contemporary popular culture does not provide the tools for understanding how the political and aesthetic interventions of feminism, anti-racism and for LGBTQ+ people affect audiences. While the packaging is capitalist, something is being sold and that something is feminist, anti-racist and LGBTQ+ positive. Side by side with individual success stories, we can find solidarity with groups of oppressed people and aesthetic innovations on their behalf. Beyoncé's aesthetic accomplishment in *Homecoming* alludes to a Black army of musicians and dancers ready to take over. Lady Gaga refuses to be a pleasing pop star, not doing the expected and taking no more 'shit' from men in her personal and professional life. Taylor Swift grows into a political activist, alluding and developing camp aesthetics in her artistic work.

In the documentaries, these political and aesthetic interventions touch their audiences affectively, and such audiences' involvement cannot be reduced to post-feminism. Without disputing those consumerist logics and the branding of feminism as a relevant dimension in the superstars' careers, I believe it is central for feminist scholars to acknowledge the doubleness of feminist superstars' contributions. When many contemporary feminist debates in politics and theory are unable to handle sexism, racism, LGBTQ+ rights and sexual violence together, Beyoncé, Lady Gaga and Taylor Swift are doing a good job with affectively connecting audiences with feminist themes, enabling affective politics in contemporary mediated music culture.

2

Narratives about gender and feminism in a music industry #MeToo petition

On 17 November 2017, an article titled 'I Never Dared to Tell – Then I Wouldn't Get To Sing' was published in *Dagens Nyheter* (2017), the largest daily newspaper in Sweden.[1] It told stories of sexism, sexual harassment and sexual violence in the music industry and was signed by famous female artists working in Sweden. At the time, 1,993 artists had signed the petition #NärMusikenTystnar (when the music stops) and fifty-three female artists were presented with their names and photos at the bottom of the three-page article.[2] It presented personal narratives and a concluding text, resembling a manifesto, on what the music industries should do to stop misconduct. The petition received more signatures after publication of the article and a lot of media attention. Some of the famous artists who signed the petition took part in the following media debate. The petition #NärMusikenTystnar had grown out of a closed Facebook group where the signatories had shared and discussed their experiences of sexism, sexual harassment and sexual violence in the music industries. It was part of a larger movement. During autumn 2017, many closed groups on Facebook discussing #MeToo were started in Sweden. Twitter, Messenger and Instagram were also used by organizers of petitions, and the public debate in different mainstream media outlets was

---

[1] https://www.dn.se/kultur-noje/jag-vagade-aldrig-beratta-da-kanske-jag-inte-skulle-fa-sjunga-mer/ (accessed 2 March 2021).

[2] The petition, and other #MeToo petitions, were presented as by 'women' in this manner. How narratives of gender are shaped in the narratives of the petition is at the centre of the analysis in this chapter. Gender is not regarded as a given category but is seen as discursively shaped in the narratives.

craving new stories on the topic daily. Celebrity survivors and celebrity perpetrators gained the most attention. In the fields of journalism, literature and the performing arts, men were being prosecuted and/or fired. The stories published in *Dagens Nyheter* were, according to the article that accompanied them, only a few out of 'hundreds' collected on Facebook by the activists behind #NärMusikenTystnar.[3]

#MeToo is an international movement against sexual harassment and sexual violence affecting women, sometimes including transwomen, in the workplace, that took on different forms in different national contexts at the time it exploded on Twitter in 2017. The #MeToo movement of 2017 is part of a larger field of feminist online activism that is ongoing. The term was coined by Black feminist activist Tarana Burke in the United States in 2006. Nothing much happened in some countries, but in others (like Sweden) there was a tidal wave of #MeToo narratives in the media, and in yet other places there have been #MeToo movements before and since 2017 – not always under that name. The US #MeToo movement's focus on celebrity in film and the performing arts set the tone for the international news cycle, especially the Harvey Weinstein case. In Sweden, the literary figure Jean-Claude Arnault's case played out in a way that resembled the Weinstein case.[4] The questions: Who did what, how should they be punished and who got hurt, were largely in focus in the media during and after #MeToo 2017. The movement succeeded in putting workplace sexism, sexual harassment and sexual violence in focus, and policy changes were made in different work sectors. Thus, #MeToo was not only a media storm but it also resulted in political change, even though it may be too soon to know the consequences of #MeToo. Later on, in the

---

[3] Exactly how many narratives were shared in the closed Facebook group is unknown since the author was not a member of that group. The group has since been deleted and only the archived material and the published article are accessible.

[4] A figure in Swedish literary circuits known for hosting a venue called Forum in Stockholm for art and literature with his spouse. He is married to Katarina Frostenson, author and 1992–2019 member of the Swedish Academy that hands out the Nobel Prize in Literature. The Arnault scandal set off a restructuring of the Swedish Academy and the Nobel Prize in Literature was cancelled in 2018. He was later tried and convicted of rape and sent to jail. In 2017, multiple women testified about sexual harassment and sexual violence by Arnault. Jenny Sundén and Susanna Paasonen (2020: 29–30) discuss the case and compare it to the Weinstein case in the United States.

Swedish media there was increased room for questioning the credibility of the survivors, and Cissi Wallin, a journalist and a high profile #MeToo activist, was tried and found guilty of defamation for accusing another journalist of rape.

Even though #MeToo has been the topic of much research since 2017, the narratives of the petitions have rarely been analysed in detail. This chapter argues that looking closer at the narratives provides an understanding of how sexism, sexual harassment and sexual violence, gender and feminism are constructed in contemporary music industry work. Such an understanding is based on sixty-four of the stories from the petition #NärMusikenTystnar, and the manifesto text published in the article that released the petition.[5] The aim is to analyse how gender, in the subjects of the narratives and the petition, is constructed; how the music industry as a working environment is described; and the feminist demands made. The strengths and weaknesses of the feminist demands also motivate the chapter to suggest some improvements to the workplace policies of the music industries, based on the narratives of the petition. The results presented here show that the construction of gendered subjectivities, 'girls/women', in the petition is double-edged: the narratives present a young and naïve survivor, and the petition is presented as signed by popular music artists who are strong women and feminists.[6]

The material used as the empirical base for this chapter is one petition, from one country, released in 2017, and does not claim to cover #MeToo or feminist media activism in general: a diverse landscape of symbolic politics that also translates into political and institutional change. Still, the themes found in #NärMusikenTystnar are neither unique nor narrow. They hold relevance for the way gender and feminism in the music industries are described and debated internationally. My analysis of the petition is framed by research about contemporary feminist media activism, a rapidly growing research field.

---

[5] The narratives of the petition were collected from the published article and from the archive of Svenskt visarkiv.
[6] With gendered subjectivities I am here discussing how subjects are constituted in the narratives as gendered. It is the representations of a gendered subject, not the actual person's experience of their subjecthood, that are analysed. Gendered subjectivities are understood as often multidimensional and as including ideas about other sociocultural categories, like age and sexuality, race and class.

A feminist queer theory approach to gender is used to grasp the centrality of heterosexuality in the construction of gender when the survivors are represented in the narratives of the petition.

Research on #MeToo, hashtag feminism and online feminist activism

The moment of the #MeToo movement in Sweden took place in late 2017, following the US #MeToo, when stories of sexism, sexual harassment and sexual violence from #MeToo petitions overflowed the media, focusing on different professional spheres and workplaces (Grubbström & Powell, 2020, Hansson, Sveningsson & Ganetz, 2021). The movement is a product of a larger feminist activist reality focusing on sexual violence and sexual harassment that predates digital media *and* is now mobilizing tools from the development of social media to support activist structures and facilitate the viral spread of this feminist critique. There have been other moments when a feminist critique of sexual harassment has been in focus. The Anita Hill scandal in the United States in 1991 was reported on all over the world and sexual harassment in the workplace was up for public scrutiny, putting issues of gender, race and power on the media agenda, and changing legislation. #MeToo can be understood in relation to the Anita Hill scandal and other scandals that have brought sexual harassment and sexual violence in the workplace to the public debate (Erlingsdóttir & Giti 2021: 2). In fact, combatting sexual harassment and sexual violence has been a cornerstone of feminist activism for half a century, where Kate Millett's *Sexual Politics* (1970) is often described as having had an important role in shifting the theoretical paradigm of feminist politics to include issues of (private) sex in (public) feminist politics.

Feminist stances on the place of sex and sexuality in feminist politics have been polarized within feminist debates; for example, in research and activism concerned with pornography and sex work from the late 1970s onward. At the centre of these debates are questions of what a woman is, and what may be harmful social and cultural practices for women. With the risk of simplifying complex feminist debates that have been running for decades, the radical feminist position has been labelled as understanding 'woman' in essential terms and pornography and sex work as 'bad for women', expressions of a harmful, structurally understood patriarchy that should be abolished (Jeffreys 2009). While sex positive, trans and postmodern feminists have argued that sex and gender are constructed, there is no 'woman' in the essential sense. Pornography and sex work have different effects and should be valued higher and organized better (Scoular 2004). Further, feminist research may combine a critique of how the sex and porn industry affect the women, men, transwomen and other genders working in them with accounts of sex workers' subjectivity, agency and multiple experiences (Scoular 2004: 349). The climate of the feminist debate has not shifted much, sex work and trans persons are still dividing feminists into 'radical' and 'postmodern'.[7] Also, the question of who is included in the category 'woman' is still relevant when white female celebrities make the slogan (#MeToo) that was coined by a Black Brooklyn feminist activist (Tarana Burke) global. Intersectional feminist critiques, as discussed in the Introduction of this book, have been directed at the #MeToo movement's representations of women. Researchers have raised questions about the role of race and minorities in #MeToo (Onwuachi-Willig 2018, Kagal, Cowan & Jawad 2019), about the taken-for-granted heterosexuality (Halberstam 2021), about the role of abilities (Haraldsdóttir 2021) and multiple gender identities (Hsu 2019).

Focusing on the potential of feminism in social media, Jenny Sundén and Susanna Paasonen (2020: 41) analysed the #MeToo movement as an example of 'affective publics' where an emotional media discussion takes hold and has the possibility to inspire social change outside the media circuit. In their work (Sundén & Paasonen 2020), they examine not only #MeToo but also several feminist tactics in social media and argue that such feminisms are symbolic and affective in nature and hold the potential to develop into civic body politics, where institutional social change can be achieved. Independent of the potential for change that #MeToo and other feminist media activism hold, it

---

[7] For example, in the recent debates about the existence of trans exclusionary radical feminists (TERFs).

seems clear that the feminist movements are being challenged, and rightly so, to bring more sociocultural categories than gender into the conversation about sexual harassment and sexual violence. White and rich women with celebrity status were the voices most heard in the media reporting on the #MeToo movement. In the petition that this chapter analyses, not all the artists pictured in the article launching the petition are white, and different music genres and generations are represented.

Social media provided the infrastructure for the #MeToo movement, because the software solutions of social media, where discussion, befriending and spreading of information in networks, were premiered. The #MeToo movement took off on Twitter and many Swedish #MeToo petitions started in Facebook groups or on Instagram. Such forms of mediated interaction have 'made' new forms of sociability possible (van Dijck 2013). Looking beyond #MeToo, feminist online activism can be understood as (1) activism in organized groups predating social media (non-governmental organizations (NGOs), shelters, educational initiatives, marches) that now use social media, and (2) types of activism that started on or with social media by remediating and widening the reach of old methods like signing lists to protest or sharing experiences of oppression in consciousness-raising groups, to making hashtags and creating flash mobs. The Women's March in January 2017 is an example of the first kind of activism where physical protests on-site were advertised, organized and reported on through social media. Later the same year, #MeToo started as a social media activist action, important within media. Both of these feminist events spread across the globe, making 2017 an important year for contemporary feminist activism. Social media is undoubtedly revitalizing feminism and redrawing the map with a transnational reach – pussyhats from the United States and dance moves from the Chilean protest 'Un violador en tu camino' are trending in many countries. Feminist political issues are old. Feminist activists have been combatting femi(ni)cide, sexual harassment and sexual violence, and fighting for reproductive rights for a long time. However, it seems uncertain if structural, institutional, long-term change can be achieved by these media activisms. The virality of feminist activist events on social media also spreads to mainstream media. Feminist social media activism therefore has the possibility to reach a large audience, even though not all initiatives do.

At the same time, 'hashtag feminism' is sometimes used in a derogatory way, accused of being a feminist action that does no more than share a hashtag on social media. The societal effects of hashtag feminism are yet to be thoroughly researched (Mendes, Ringrose & Keller 2018). Nevertheless, #MeToo has put sexual violence and sexual harassment on the agenda, perpetrators in jail and forced governments and businesses to discuss policy and practice in the workplace. It seems timely to ask what social media has done for feminism and look at the pros and cons of the 2010s social media feminist movements. The focus of this chapter will be on one particular case: #NärMusikenTystnar.

The stories told

In the winter of 2019, fifty-two stories from #NärMusikenTystnar were anonymously archived by Svenskt visarkiv, a government agency that 'collects, preserves and publishes materials in the fields of traditional folk, older popular music, Swedish jazz, traditional and social dance and emerging new traditions'.[8] At Svenskt visarkiv, they believed that the #MeToo movement was an interesting aspect of musical life in Sweden that should be preserved for future generations in their public archives. Together with the administrators of the music, performing arts and comedy #MeToo petitions, Svenskt visarkiv set up a system to digitally archive the stories of sexual harassment and sexual violence.[9] All stories archived at Svenskt visarkiv are anonymous, approved to be archived by the narrators themselves and sent in to the archive by the administrators of the petitions. The archived #MeToo stories are accessible to the public on request. The number of stories that were part of the original #NärMusikenTystnar petition on Facebook is unknown; however, the article mentions hundreds. Twelve additional unique stories can be found in the

---

[8] https://musikverket.se/svensktvisarkiv/?lang=en (accessed 12 March 2021).
[9] Working in the archives, I also had access to archived stories from three other petitions: #TystnadTagning (film and performing arts), #SkrattetIHalsen (stand-up comedians) and #MeTooBackstage (the backstage workers of film and the performing arts). These are not analysed here. Two other (smaller) music-focused petitions were involved in discussions with the archive but their stories were never archived.

article that launched the petition. The narrators of those twelve stories did not approve them for archiving, but as they are in the published article they are still publicly preserved. The sixty-four stories (in total) and the text published in the article that frames the stories are the material analysis dealt with in this chapter.

I employ a thematic analysis (King & Horrocks 2010: 152, Braun & Clark 2006) to investigate what is said in the material from the petition. The methodological approach builds on identifying, analysing and describing patterns in the material at hand (Braun & Clark 2006: 79). Following the thematic analysis, a discourse theoretical approach is used, understanding language as constituting a reality, rather than being the consequence of a reality (Potter & Wetherell 1987). Thus, the texts analysed in this chapter are not seen as reflecting reality but constructing it by leaving things out, highlighting other things, describing them in certain ways, and so on. Arguing that language constitutes reality does not negate the experiences of sexual harassment and sexual violence told, rather it directs our focus to the constitution of gender, the workplaces of the music industries and the feminism present in #MeToo. When thematizing the stories about experiences of sexism, sexual harassment and sexual violence, I study how the narrator's gender is described and what other subjects are constructed in the stories, what place and time the experience plays out in, the roles and professions of the subjects involved and the descriptions of the music industries and music work. Characteristics, behaviours, feelings and narrative tropes that occur often in the material are drawn out as themes. These themes structure the following analysis where the materials constituting representations of age, gender, music and the music industries are developed. In the final part of the chapter, I turn to the feminist demands of the manifesto in the newspaper article that launched #NärMusikenTystnar. These are discussed in light of the findings in the stories and compared with previous research on sexual harassment and sexual violence. I believe that it is important to critically discuss what survivors and perpetrators are described in the #MeToo petition, how the effects of the sexual harassment and sexual violence and the music industries are constituted, what type of change is suggested for the music industries and what effects the suggested actions may produce.

The young survivor

The analysis that follows focuses first on the sixty-four stories of lived experiences of sexism, sexual harassment and sexual violence, investigating themes that were identified in the narratives by asking questions about who, what, where, when and how the abuse took place. Age and age difference, the gendering of the subjects represented in the narratives, loving music and working in music, the time and place of the incidents and finally the feminist demands put forward in the petition structure the analysis. In the conclusion, the gendering of young survivors and grown-up feminists, in the narratives and through the signatories to the petition, is discussed as two subject positions inhabited by (possibly) the same popular music artists.

Starting with the theme of age and age difference, a majority of the sixty-four narratives mentioned the age of the survivor and/or perpetrator directly or indirectly. Thus, age by its presence in most stories seemed to carry meaning for how sexism, sexual harassment and sexual violence are constructed as part of the work environment of music work. In one of the experiences, the narrator/survivor describes their internship at a 'cool' independent record label. The owner of the label calls the narrator, seventeen to eighteen years old, sexy and good looking and the situation escalates over time. This is how it is told:

> This happened when I was between 17 and 18 and had an internship at one of the 'cool' independent record labels. I was so very happy and pleased to have gotten an internship at that label and already on the first day I was met by this owner of the label. It started already that week when he mostly made comments in front of others sitting in the same office as me that I was good looking and sexy and that he would like to take me out on a date and so on. Then it continued [. . .] every time my friend was in the bathroom or running errands, he closed the door on us two in his office and told me that he wanted to fuck me then and there on the floor and asked if we should do it. I felt really bad but didn't dare to tell my friend who was with me. I felt bad for not saying no, I felt and thought all the time 'I am agreeing to this because I am not putting my foot down, it's my own fault'. Finally, it came to this idiot telling me and my friend to come to his place to work there and

when we were on our way, he called my friend to send her on a long errand in the city, but I should come. I came to his house, and we were sitting on his sofa, and I had a computer doing something. Finally, he grabbed me and told me that he had wanted me for so long. He pushed me down into the sofa and I ended up on my hands and knees. He pulled my pants off and had anal sex with me (I'm not sure for how long because I passed out). I passed out and woke up when the doorbell rang. I put my pants on and sat down, didn't understand anything and never wanted to tell anyone what had happened. At that moment I started denying it and pushing it away.[10]

I will return to several aspects of this narrative in the following discussion. First, I would like to highlight that many stories from the #NärMusikenTystnar petition (and other petitions I have read) are horrible. Reading and analysing them was not an easy task and it is important that the narratives' contents are not naturalized. With that said, I believe it is important for the reader to read them to be able to better understand what is at stake for survivors of sexual harassment and sexual violence in the music industries. A central part of this first story is that the narrator is young and new to the music industries as this is their first internship. In many of the narratives, the narrators are constituted as young, starting their careers at the time of the assaults, while the perpetrators are often described as older, sometimes the same age but never younger than the survivor. The combination of young survivors who do not yet know the music business and feel insecure and the use of the past tense in the language of the narrative constructs the survivor as older now, in the present. Some stories mention the age of the survivor with a number: 'we were 16–17 and played at a big festival'; 'I was 23 when a juror from one of the biggest talent-shows called me'. Here are two other examples where a numerical age is given and holds significance for the narrative:

A drummer, a middle-aged man, wondered backstage how old I was. I answered and told him that I was 15 years old, and he said, 'then you're old enough to come home to my place for a sweet weekend treatment, I can

---

[10] The archived narratives are translated by the author from Swedish to English and kept as true as possible to the original language. The whole narratives of each story are included with some minor omissions.

teach you how to fuck'. I was perplexed and mumbled 'no thank you' and hurried away.

Two persons, one a roadie and the other one a member of an American rock band assaulted me. I was 20 years old at the time and afterwards they told me that I'm pretty ok but it's a shame that I don't have a flat tummy when the rest of my body is ace. Their review of the rape damaged my body image. It took me many years to tell my friends why they had to wait for me that morning, why I was late for the ride home.

The narrative examples given thus far have shown that the age of the survivors is given importance in the narratives. Age is also constructed indirectly. One narrator is described as 'not knowing how to drink coffee yet', one is returning home to their parents' house and several mention school situations: both in high schools and higher music education. The situations described also help constitute the survivors as young at the time of their described experiences of sexism, sexual harassment and sexual violence. They are performing for the first time at a major event, a festival, doing a photo shoot for their first album or meeting an agent to start their career. One narrative about promotional work for a first album states:

> 'Lick your lips and part them – that works.' I'm at the photo shoot for my first album and the record company boss gives me input.

Youth, implicit inexperience of sex and explicit inexperience of music industry work are therefore important factors in constructing the narratives of sexual harassment and sexual assault, but it is not any type of youth. The survivors are feminized by being described as 'sexy', 'good looking' and 'naïve', words connoting young femininity. One story describes the other side of the youth-focused sexism of the music industries:

> And then there was him at the record company that I got to present my music to. He listened and said that this was good but you have to understand that if we sign an artist she has to be able to sit on TV sofas and look good and you are not really 20.

Constructing young femininity as 'looking good', being sexually desirable and especially appealing to older men is at the core of the heterosexual fantasy of mainstream popular culture. Rosalind Gill has argued (2007: 218) that Western popular culture is obsessed with heterosexual romance, a romance shaped by power and by the represented differences in masculinities and femininities. A foundational idea in feminist queer theory is that cultural gender ideals are constructed in terms of sexuality and race, as not only binary in opposites of male/female but also seeing those categories as desiring each other and naturalizing racial (kinship) order (de Lauretis 1987). Feminist critiques of sexism in narratives built on feminine teenage beauty as desirable exist in relation to film, consider *American Beauty*, and popular music, consider Vanessa Paradis or Britney Spears. The popular cultural construction of femininity is also a construction of heterosexual desire for young femininity by older men, establishing a clear difference and a power imbalance as the base of heterosexual desire.[11] In such a reading, the 'beautiful young girl/woman' reveals how normative ideas of age and looks constitute femininity as heterosexually desirable at a young age, not in old age. #MeToo can be understood as the 'beautiful young woman' speaking back, her claiming her subjecthood and narrating her own story. But the narratives can also be understood as reassuring the audience of the centrality of the 'beautiful young woman' for the construction of gender and heteronormative desire in the music industries. #NärMusikenTystnar constructs the heterosexual desire for young femininity as central, yet with negative implications for culture. In a similar vein, Jack Halberstam (2021: 183) has argued that the heterosexuality constructed in the #MeToo movement is dependent on differences between men and women. Those differences are constructing a heterosexuality that becomes toxic, where powerful men abuse and (most) women succumb to the practice (ibid.). The idea of the beautiful young woman who is also a talented musician and lifted up – to fame – by a more experienced man with whom she is in a heterosexual relationship or having a romance with, is not new. The narrative can be seen in films like *A Star Is Born*, *Walk the Line* and *Tina: What's Love Got To Do with It*. Power imbalances and differences between the

---

[11] Gender and heterosexuality as linked has been theorized by scholars like Gloria Anzaldúa (1991), Teresa De Lauretis (1987) and Judith Butler (1990).

male/female subjects of a romance are a continuum to heterosexual abuse (Halberstam 2021). Thus, the age difference portrayed in the narratives of #NärMusikenTystnar analysed here plays into an already given construction of heterosexuality where (older) more experienced men desire (younger) beautiful women. In this heterosexual idea, femininities are at a disadvantage in power, experience and strength, a disadvantage that is a gendered construction where the youth gives gender meaning. The narrators talking to us now, those depicted in the article launching the petition have experience and a position from which to speak. The subjects described in the stories did not speak back at the time. With some exceptions, most of the first persons in the narratives tried to forget, tried not to hear and blamed themselves. It is therefore not the same subject position that is described in the narratives, as now they are speaking back.

Gendering survivors and perpetrators

So far, I have discussed how the traits of youth, beauty and sexiness are feminized in the stories through the narrative of the young woman and how she is sexually harassed, abused or raped by the more experienced older man. While the perpetrators are pointed out as men by being called him/man/older man/male producer/male artist and repertoire (A&R) agent and so on, the survivors in the narratives are rarely described as female.[12] Since the narratives analysed are written in the first person and the narrator is anonymous, the gender of the narrator is often lost. This would have been different in the original context of the Facebook group because the narrators would have been revealed with their name and photo. There are some exceptions: in one story a narrator describes being called 'our own bitch' and she is gendered by the insult; one states that she was 'invited as a girl, not as an equal'. In the stories of rape, the feminization of being young, pretty and raped is achieved without mentioning gender. This happens in the first story cited here, and the

---

[12] With a few exceptions, as in the story on the previous page where the narrator is gendered 'she'.

second and third stories (above). Since women are perceived as being more rape-able than men in heterosexual culture, and as being more closely related to female dogs, 'bitch', the gender of the narrator is understood without being mentioned. If it was a young and pretty man who was being raped or called a bitch, such a storyline would require a mention of his gender and possibly his sexuality in order for the story to make sense. A rape, further, is labelled as anal in the first narrative. This is required because using only the term 'rape' implies vaginal rape. Mentioning that the rape was an 'anal rape' also enforces the female gendering of the narrator. By stating that the narrator was raped anally without mentioning the gender or the sexuality of the narrator, a vaginal rape is constructed possible, therefore the narrator is a woman (with a vagina). In another rape narrative there is also no mention of the survivor's gender. It is through the cultural understanding of rape survivors as women that we understand the narrator as female if nothing else is said:

> I heard that an often-contracted music producer from London was interested and wanted to meet when he was in Stockholm. He was DJing at a trendy night club and put me on the list. I went, alone and nervous. After the DJ set, he wanted to drop his equipment off at the hotel room and asked me to come with him, after we would go out and eat something and talk. Stupid and hopeful – I went with him. He was namedropping a lot, promised me the world etcetera etcetera, and . . . took off my clothes. I tried to wiggle my way out of it, but he held on really hard. He raped me on the carpet. I was wearing white socks. Remember how sperm ran down my legs, on the carpet, on the socks and it hurt so fucking bad. He went all night. Lost count.

In this narrative, as in the first and third stories cited in this chapter, there are no language clues to the gender of the survivor. It is the rape of a 'stupid and hopeful' person by a music producer who is constructed as male (he). Still, in the context of the mostly female artists who signed the petition, and the photos of female artists in the article launching it, survivors are also constructed as women. It seems likely that some of these signatories and artists in the photos are the narrators of the stories. Their gender also becomes self-evident in the context of #MeToo 2017, they *do not have to* point out that they are women.

A study of sexual violence at live music events in the UK has concluded (Hill, Hesmondhalgh & Megson 2020) that sexual violence at music events has negative effects on the experiences of music and health, and that the sexual violence mainly affects women while most perpetrators are men. In recent research on sexual violence in music, the survivors have also been gendered female. A study of sexual violence at Australian music festivals reached female survivors as participants (Fileborn, Wadds & Tomson 2020: 199). This was despite the study design inviting 'men and gender-diverse people' as participants too. Gendering the survivors of sexual harassment and sexual violence in the music industries as female is, despite this evidence, performative. That is, other survivors are hidden from view by describing survivors as women. The gendering of the survivor as young and female in the petition analysed here not only points to a gender-based problem *but* it also helps construct sexual harassment and sexual violence as a problem reserved for beautiful young women, newcomers to the music industries. While I am not disputing that these subjects are at risk, others may be at risk too.

Another prominent narrative starting point, repeated in the stories of #NärMusikenTystnar, is the narrator being in a group of men. Here, the survivor is gendered female by the backdrop of 'men in groups' and how they are gendered. Men in groups are described as gendered subjects in a negative manner: they are sexist, loud and support each other. The experiences described in the sixty-four stories, as stated before, range from sexism and sexual harassment to assault and rape. Men in groups are often described as encouraging sexist jargon, as in this example:

> On tour with only men. One of the band members buys a porn magazine and they all sit around looking at it the rest of the journey, they laugh out loud and comment on women's bodies. I try to say something, but all they do is laugh at me.

Narratives like this one about a tour construct the work environment of music work as promoting a homosocial milieu where sexist jargon about (absent) women is impossible to contest. Porn is one way that sexist jargon can be furthered and visiting strip clubs with colleagues is another example of how, in music industry workplaces, heterosexual males in groups look at women, as in this narrative:

> The marketing chief at a major label who thinks it's appropriate to invite the whole label to a sex club during the summer party. I feel unsure if I should go or not, I am new, I don't know how it works, maybe this is normal? He comes up to me, holds me and says 'you're coming right? Just wanted to let you know it's pretty hardcore'. I decide not to go to the party. The same boss talked to my boobs instead of me, groped numerous employees, the female artists. Management found out about what happened at the events over and over without doing shit. 'He was just a bit drunk'. Instead, he got a promotion. Hurray!

In this story, the focus is on one man, the marketing chief, and how his sexism and sexual harassment are tolerated by others. He is enabled by an unnamed group that follows him to the sex club and makes excuses for him after incidents. The collective of supporters is not gendered here, but given the dominance of men on the staff of record labels and the gendering of the artists he groped, his supporters are indirectly constructed as men. As the end of the story indicates, his behaviour is not deemed a serious problem by management, it was a drunken mishap. Similar situations with musicians, several men, streaking on tour or watching porn together in a hotel room show that sexist jargon, porn consumption and sex clubs are described as part of the music industries, not as exceptions. Without judging people who watch porn, a professional work environment is ruled by laws on discrimination and sexual harassment that make porn a problem. In Sweden, the law defines sexual harassment as 'Besides comments and words, this [sexual harassment] could involve unwanted touching or leering. It could also be a question of unwelcome compliments, invitations or insinuations.'[13] In Swedish law, it is important that the perpetrator is told that their behaviour is unwanted and experienced as harassment; however, 'In certain circumstances the offensive nature of the behaviour may be so obvious that no comment is required from the victim'.[14] It is clear from the narrative above that he was reported to management on several occasions, and therefore there is no question

---

[13] For an explanation of the whole law, see https://www.do.se/other-languages/english/what-is-discrimination/#10 (accessed 24 June 2021).

[14] https://www.do.se/other-languages/english/what-is-discrimination/#10 (accessed 24 June 2021).

about the 'unwanted-ness' of his behaviour. The tolerance for sexist jargon and porn described in the narratives, and the excuses made for men in the work environments of the music industries construct them as unwelcoming places. In the narratives, most survivors lack their own support groups, and if they describe having friends it is commonly stated that they did not tell their friends about the sexism, sexual harassment or sexual violence, as seen in the analysis of the rape narratives above. Men are both gendered with pronouns and described clearly as negatively masculine in the stories. This is culturally unusual since white heterosexual men's (the lack of discussion of race and sexuality renders them as such by default) masculinity is often invisible and naturalized in popular culture and popular music.

Gender – again

Other sociocultural aspects of the survivors' and perpetrators' constructed subjectivity – such as class, ethnicity, race and sexuality – are not present in the narratives. Neither are other forms of discrimination, like racism or homophobia. While the narrators' subjectivities in the stories are gendered young, female and heterosexual, their class, ethnicity and race also warrant discussion. The language is Swedish, the context is the music industries and besides a mention of perpetrators being from London or America and one of the narratives describing being on tour abroad when reporting an attempted rape, the stories seem to (implicitly) portray Sweden. Besides the mention of Stockholm, a Swedish award gala and a Swedish talent show, most stories do not paint a picture of the national context, the nationality of the subjects or the ethnicity or race of either survivor or perpetrator. A study (Baker et al. 2020) on how the media portrayed sexual assault in the music industries in late 2017 after #meNOmore – the music industry petition in Australia – showed that the survivors reported on were portrayed as 'privileged white attractive female music superstars' (Baker et al. 2020: 202). The artists in the photos of the article launching #NärMusikenTystnar include Black artists, indigenous artists and artists with parents who immigrated to Sweden, even if most of the artists photographed for the article are white and born in Sweden. Still, the stories are painting a picture where race, ethnicity, sexuality, class and so on are not significant in sexual harassment and sexual violence, a picture where assault is related to gender, age and beauty but no other power trajectories. In this simple (but effective) construction of sexual violence, all the perpetrators are constructed as male and all the survivors are constructed as female. In one of the stories, a survivor uses alleged homosexuality to get away from a man who is harassing her. Being gay is described as something she claims to be to get out of an uncomfortable situation. Thus, the story constructs her as heterosexual. Since the stories focus solely on sexual harassment and sexual violence as gender based and heterosexual, they are hiding other possible dimensions. Sundén and Paasonen (2020: 43) argue that the binary gender construction of #MeToo is omitting people 'differently gendered, classed, raced or sexualized', and that this is a rhetorical strength of the movement because it makes the message easy to understand. But when those different experiences are excluded from feminist movements, there is a risk of creating a feminism that is not for everyone (ibid.). Gender and age stand alone as explanations of power, discrimination and abuse in the music industries. There is no reason to believe that racism, homophobia and transphobia are not present in these workplaces, affecting the workings of sexism, sexual harassment and sexual violence in the music industries (Svensson 2020).

Loving music in the workplaces of the music industries

In the stories, the reason given for the survivors being in the situations where sexism, sexual harassment and sexual violence occur is the longing to sing and play music. Loving music, being naïve and having dreams of singing and playing are reasons that repeat themselves in the stories of sexual harassment and sexual violence. One narrator phrased it like this:

> One of my earliest music producers, a bluesman. I was still a teenager. He started sexualizing me in the studio during recording. For example: I am singing, and he tells me in the headphones over talk back 'when you sing the word "hard" sexy like that I get fucking hard'. It went on. My singing made

him horny he let me know. I just wanted to sing and be the best. A childhood dream.

Similar motives can be seen in the narratives discussed previously in this chapter. One survivor is happy about an internship at a 'cool' label, one wants to work with a famous producer, one is new to her record company job. Another narrator writes in her story that: 'all I wanted was to live for music – the price I had to pay was being scared every time I worked'. The driving force is described as wanting to sing and loving music. The ambition to be a star, famous, rich or a celebrity is not put forward in the narratives, but making it in the music industries also involves these aspects.

In the narratives, the narrators are attracted to their workplaces by their love of music, but the workplaces are described as ruled by men in power positions, by bosses, agents, bookers and so on. In the petition's narratives, the perpetrators in power do not have pleasant or humanizing characteristics. One perpetrator used to be a friend until he tries to repeatedly kiss and grope the narrator. But his friendliness is described as not his true self. Despite their unsympathetic portrayal, perpetrators are also shaped by the bystanders, fans, colleagues and bosses who stand by them and defend them. The idea of the genius as (implicitly) male has been deconstructed (Battersby 1989), and the idea of geniuses as male is central to the construction of a musical canon (Citron 1993). In popular music research concerned with sexual assault, Catherine Strong and Emma Rush (2018) discuss how well-known persons guilty of violence against women in popular music history, using Phil Spector as an example, are presented in narratives where they are constructed as musical geniuses. Strong and Rush problematize the tension between genius and rapist/murderer and discuss how to address such figures in mediated popular music history. They (2018: 577) conclude that the reason popular music history may shy away from mentioning a genius artist's 'violence against women' may be that there is a risk of ruining the musical pleasure for the fans. They argue that acknowledging sexual violence, femi(ni)cide and sexual harassment is central to writing ethical music history. Thus, they argue that the abusive artist should be written about, but their dark side must be included. In research about the intersections of gender and race in #MeToo, Rebecca Leung and

Robert Williams (2019: 356) highlight the importance of fans' support for sexual predators, here R Kelly and Bill Cosby, by discussing if the survivors should be believed, and in supporting their heroes fans become enablers (ibid.: 354). Their findings indicate that it takes more than a single event for an artist perceived as a genius to be understood as a predator in public opinion, because of the attachments people have to the music and the artist. In fact, not even overwhelming evidence may for sure 'cancel' (Clark 2020) a musical genius. This discursive idea about musical talent and geniuses applies to artists, but producers and record company founders can also be understood through this narrative where the genius can either do no wrong or is excused from what he is doing due to his genius position. In the narratives of the petition at hand, these ideas about men in the music industries are not described explicitly, rather they are background knowledge that helps us to understand how the perpetrators are allowed to behave the way they do in the narratives. The cultural idea of a male genius colours the work environments of music.

While many of the narrators are describing their dreams of singing and making it in the music industries, they appear to have continued working in music because of how the stories are told – 'my first album/festival/show' implies that more followed. There are also a few narratives where the narrator leaves the music industries due to their experiences of workplace sexual harassment and sexual violence.

> I was a musician/singer on a tour when I was about 20. Young and naive and in the beginning of my freelance career, at least that was what I hoped for and believed. But it didn't take long until it was obvious that I was there because I was a girl, young, good looking and assumed willing. Who wouldn't put out if it meant more shows? After many advances, hands in the wrong places, tongues against my skin, whispered promises about my own contract if I only . . . . I chose to leave the world that I had dreamt to be a part of since I was a child.

This narrator describes being disillusioned with music work and walking away from the initial 'dream' that brought them there. Giving up on the dream completely is unusual. More commonly, the narrators stay in the music industries, but their own careers suffer after they are sexually harassed or abused. One of the more striking examples includes a narrator who recounts being raped by a famous male musician and states in the story that she 'lost a lot of friends'. Those friends are described as not wanting to cut their ties with the rapist because of his influence in the business. In this narrative being raped was bad for her career, but not for the rapist's career. Another story describes a survivor who calls being raped a hindrance to her career, because her rapist bad-mouthed her and being freelance she had a hard time getting work. Even if one does not complain, being abused is described as leading to professional punishment for the survivors in the workplaces of the music industries. This story may be a clue to how retaliation functions:

> As one of a few female agents and at a major label I can't even try to remember all the comments female artists get that are unrelated to their music. I think about a famous female artist where I, really, was told that she had slept with the whole business including the man who told me. (I said 'good for her' and 'you would have never told me if she was a man'. Afterwards: I wonder if those experiences were voluntary?)

This narrator is pointing to the possibility that the sexual experiences of a female artist that are described as consensual might really be rapes. Thus, a raped female artist could be called a slut in the workplace since the gendered expectations of women illustrated in the story are that they should not sleep around. This risk of being labelled a slut and not believed gives the survivors a good reason to stay quiet. In the stories where the survivors do report the sexual crimes to the police, or tell others, these attempts are described as unsuccessful in leading to punishment for the perpetrators. Rather, their own careers suffer when they talk about the assaults. The narratives repeat that the consequences of talking about or reporting the sexual harassment and sexual violence were at best nothing, and at worst had further negative effects on the survivors. Sara Ahmed (2012) has argued that when a person exposes a problem in the workplace (discussing racism), that person poses a problem, and getting rid of them may seem to be the solution. She suggests that through this logic, persons who speak up about injustice in workplaces are often punished for doing so. The petition #NärMusikenTystnar and the article launching it are not only putting sexism, sexual harassment and sexual violence in focus, but also critiquing the practice of punishing survivors who speak up. #MeToo is exposing a problem in the workplace, but with the collective and anonymous voices behind the large number of stories and signatories it can prevent repercussions for single individuals.[15]

Narrating time and place

All the stories discussed here are told in the past tense, as something that happened before. The phrasing describes the stories as happening a long time ago: 'I was young', 'it was at our first festival', 'my first photo shoot' and other narrative tropes that construct time as having passed. The exact time of the events is rarely given – in one story the year of an award gala where abuse happened is mentioned. A clue to the temporal context of the narratives could be their lack of home studios, social media and smartphones. The petition came about because of the development of web 2.0 and social media, but these are not part of the narratives. This puts the stories in a reality before recent digital media development, and is an indicator that they happened a while back. It could also be that they are described as happening outside of media. Having your own home studio may lead to independence from producers and bosses presented as perpetrators, but it may also mean that you have to invite them into your home. Returning to the youth of the survivors, the temporality of the stories combined with the youth of the survivors paints a gendered timeline. Where teenagers are innocent, the older artists signing the petition are no longer girls, but women uncovering the truth of a gendered system of sexual violence.

Certain places frequent the narratives of #NärMusikenTystnar more than others. The places where sexual violence takes place include the homes of the perpetrators, hotel rooms, parties and after parties, tours (including buses, dressing rooms and backstage areas), studios and the stage itself. Sexual

---

[15] Nevertheless, individuals have been punished for speaking up in the #MeToo movement as well. In the Swedish context, most famously Cissi Wallin. https://www.thelocal.se/20191209/swedish-metoo-activist-told-to-pay-damages-to-man-she-accused-of-rape/ (accessed 29 June 2021).

harassment and sexism can takes place in less private settings such as photo shoots, in everyday conversations or at meetings, to name a few examples. Other components of the incidents described are the presence of alcohol and being drugged, as well as being passed out or asleep or passing out during a sexual assault. While this feature of the narratives may not be surprising, it seems relevant to discuss that certain environments are described as less safe than others. It seems insufficient to recommend artists to avoid these situations. Despite the obvious problem with such advice, the victim should not have to limit their life. What would be the effect on artists' careers if they cannot have one-on-one meetings with a manager, producer or record company boss? Or if they cannot attend events that serve alcohol? Actions against sexual harassment and sexual violence that combat risk environments may therefore lead to negative effects for potential victims of sexual harassment or sexual violence – since the workforce of the music industries is not likely to stop partying. Policy against alcohol may just move the party out of reach for some persons more than others, discriminating against them in a different way. If a new employee chooses not to attend the summer party for fear of sexism and abuse (as in the example above with the sex club), she also misses out on networking opportunities. If the party is forbidden by workplace policy, some colleagues might go anyway but in a smaller more exclusive group, still networking. The discussion on how to handle the implications of the stories becomes relevant in the light of the actions against sexual harassment and sexual violence that are proposed by the petition in the newspaper article. They will be further discussed below in the final part of the analysis.

Feminist demands

Thus far, the discussion has focused on the stories of experiences of sexism, sexual harassment and sexual violence, what they say about gender and what ideas about gender they portray. At the end of the article in *Dagens Nyheter* (2017) that launched the petition #NärMusikenTystnar, a list of demands and some statements were included as well as a short text explaining that the signatories of the petition had had enough. The first demand is for zero tolerance of 'sexual abuse and violence', where all such conduct should lead to the termination of employment in the music industries. The second demand is that stakeholders, bosses and decision-makers in the music industries should carry the responsibility, also stating that they have failed. These two demands are followed by more general statements that 'we' will listen to each other and find support in the stories told and place the shame where it belongs: with the perpetrators and the bystanders. Finally, the signatories state that they speak with one voice, will not comment on this article, that 'a no is a no' and that 'we' know who 'you' are. The last sentence could be read as a threat to reveal the names of the perpetrators, names that may have been circulated in the closed Facebook group but are not shown in the article.

The three main demands – terminating the contracts of perpetrators, placing the responsibility on those in power and talking about the problems – are well-known suggestions for how change can be achieved in organizations. The first two focus on individuals; if perpetrators are fired, bosses and the people holding power take responsibility things will improve. The third focuses instead on a collective conducting a conversation about the issues. The music industries include many freelance positions and short-term contracts. The first demand for zero tolerance seems to assume that the perpetrators have contracts that could be terminated. That is true for a record label executive or an A&R agent but not for most touring musicians and studio staff. A person with a permanent contract, however, cannot be fired because of one incident of sexual harassment. Swedish law makes the employer, not the employees, responsible for workplace sexual harassment and the employer is responsible to rehabilitate, investigate and prevent. Some of the situations described in the narratives could land the perpetrators in jail. If one is convicted of rape, then firing that person is possible, depending on the employer's policy. But the conviction rate for rape is not high. The demand for zero tolerance is understandable given the horrific stories in the petition. But the signatories display a low degree of knowledge about workplace policies and laws regulating sexual harassment and sexual violence.

The second demand, that the stakeholders take responsibility, does not formulate clear action or a way forward. Putting the responsibility on those in power could make managers revisit their policies on gender and diversity, and their general work environment policy. However, not all stakeholders have formal positions, and one difficulty therefore is how to approach the informal power held by male geniuses without management positions (producers, artists and agents, for example) and demand they take responsibility. In order for powerful individuals in the music industries to stop supporting persons who are guilty of sexual harassment and sexual violence, one must assume that the realization (with them) of the harm it causes overrides their friendships and the profit-oriented goals. The stories emphasize that it is the people with formal and informal power who are the perpetrators. Thus, they are the bosses or persons the bosses know or depend on. This may make the second demand tricky: Can perpetrators be expected to take responsibility? The third suggested action, rather than a demand, is to keep the conversation going and believe in each other. As a feminist method, consciousness raising, discussing the issues of sexual harassment and sexual violence among those exposed, could potentially change organizational culture. Talking and listening, believing and afterwards acting to make the music industries better workplaces could lead to change. It could create a climate where acting against misconduct becomes normal, instead of the opposite. This approach would also allow for differences within the industries, where the problems lie in record companies, tour management and other professional fields, to appear. Local solutions and grounded courses of action against sexual harassment and sexual violence could be taken in collaboration.

The three main demands/suggestions presented in the petition do not seem to present us with tools to promote institutional change. In related work in the Swedish performing arts, a national policy work commission has been working with all major unions and theatre stages since 2017 to prevent sexual harassment in the performing arts.[16] It is now common on movie sets to have an intimacy coordinator, a person monitoring the sex and nude scenes with the aim of preventing any sexual misconduct. Other policy change has been implemented and a collective ongoing strategy has been built. After #MeToo, seminars directed at people working in music were held, for example by

---

[16] https://scenochfilm.se/wp-content/uploads/2018/04/rapport_ett_tillfalle_att_ta_vara_pa_webb.pdf is a Swedish version of their report.

Musiksverige, but a broad initiative against sexual harassment and sexual violence in the music industries, including the diverse organizations that make up the Swedish music industries, is missing.

Previous research reviewing Nordic studies on sexual harassment in the workplace has found that young women are over-represented as survivors (Svensson 2020: 53). Also, previous qualitative studies have shown that survivors who experience sexual harassment and sexual violence in the workplace at a young age, do not recognize the experiences as such until they are older (Blackstone, Houle & Uggen 2014). From the preceding analysis, it is clear what subjects are seen as most at risk and what places and events are perceived as risky. Conclusions drawn from the stories could be that if there are no young unaccompanied artists working in music, no drugs or alcohol in the work environment, no closed sessions with only two participants in homes or studios, sexual harassment and violence would drastically decline. Working in the music industries, and other entertainment industries, pose risks because of the thin line between work space and private space and the power some hold over many individual careers. Acknowledging the risks and adopting policies addressing age, parties and one-on-one sessions for all artists would simultaneously prevent sexual harassment and sexual violence facing all genders and prevent the discrimination of young women. If policy only targets young women, they risk being excluded from career-promoting activities. However, targeting the possible predators instead, would be another route to follow, curtailing the power of single individuals. As previously pointed out, power imbalances related to class, ethnicity, race, sexuality and so on may also put some persons more at risk. For music industry policy to address this, young artists should be handled by a professional system, not by their parents, and power dimensions intersecting with gender (such as race and racism) should also be addressed when combatting sexual harassment and sexual violence.

Conclusion

The subjects put forward in #NärMusikenTystnar are both the survivors described in the stories, the beautiful young girls assumed white and heterosexual, *and* the signatories, the female artists signing the petition, presumably some of them have also written the narratives. These two subject positions, the survivor and the signing feminist, are constituted in different ways by the stories and the demands of the petition. Using the lens of queer theory (de Lauretis 1987, Butler 1990, Halberstam 2021), these gendered subject positions are performative – they create ideas about gender through sexuality, femininity and Swedish-ness. The survivors' innocence and dreams of musical success are important for the stories and recreate a feminine gendered stereotype. The signatories represent a different subject position. With their demands and the action of putting the petition forward, they have uncovered the truth about the music industries and are no longer innocent. Their position as 'feminists' reveals gender-based sexual abuse in the music industries, places the blame on the perpetrator, makes demands and speaks up, and by these traits the signatories are presented as gendered in a way juxtaposed with the survivor in the narratives. The split between how the types of femininities of the young 'survivor' of the past and the 'feminist' of the present are constituted enables the #MeToo petition to present females in the music industries as both. There is both a vulnerable female victim to protect, and a strong woman who speaks up for her.

The networked media is the infrastructure that provides a base for these multiple femininities to be presented. Zizi Papacharissi (2012) argues that presentations of the self on social media – in her example Twitter – are networked performances and must therefore contain polysemic content. As Twitter, Facebook and Instagram are the social media used by the #MeToo movement, their representations obey the logics of networked media in how subject positions are multiple. Social media provides an opportunity to create content that can easily spread (Jenkins, Ford & Green 2013). The #MeToo movement's success in making narratives of sexual harassment and sexual violence heard would not have been possible without Twitter and the spread of the hashtag. The petition analysed here would not have started if the hashtag had not spread. Thus, the polysemic subjects and spreadable messages of social media are foundational for the feminist demands made on the music industries.

Finally, a risk of the petition's construction of the beautiful young woman, as noted before, is that the subject position may come through strongly to audiences, be associated with sexual harassment and preserve the idea that the survivor of sexual harassment and sexual violence is a certain type of woman: young, pretty, heterosexual, white and so on. If one looks closer at a petition like #NärMusikenTystnar, the feminist subject position of the signatories *also* furthers the success story of contemporary feminist media activism promoting agency in women. Women who are diverse in their presentation, in generation, age, race/ethnicity and sexuality. Neither of the subject positions is constructed as bad or guilty of anything, rather the co-existence of the survivor and the feminist shows that multiple femininities can take place in #MeToo, widening and deepening the performative gender politics of the petition. Its strength is exactly that: letting women in the music industries be young, stupid, sad, angry, feminist and demanding in the same petition. This is an achievement of #MeToo that is obscured if we do not read the narratives that built it and only look at the movement as presented on the cover of magazines.

3

Gender equality, diversity and algorithmic culture on music streaming services

In the autumn of 2018, I was presenting my research on how gendering takes place on the music streaming service Spotify (Werner 2020b) at a conference when a colleague and friend brought my attention to an online tool for music listeners: 'The Smirnoff Equalizer', and showed me how it worked on his computer screen. The equalizer was a tool with its own website created by Smirnoff and Spotify and placed within Smirnoff's initiative 'Smirnoff equalizing music'.[1] With the equalizer, Smirnoff and Spotify were aiming to equalize music listening between 'men and women artists' by analysing the listening patterns of accounts, displaying how many 'women' and 'men' artists were listened to and then giving a value judgement (e.g. my friend received: 'Great! You listen to more women artists than the average'). The equalizer would then suggest a playlist where the listener could adjust the percentage of 'women' artists included.

I found the gender equality software solution sported by two large commercial companies, selling alcohol and music subscriptions, fascinating. The equalizer, I thought, is an example of music streaming services not only representing and constructing gender with software, but also making conscious efforts to promote software for gender equality. The equalizer (2018–20) was an intervention addressing the topic of gender equality in music listening, a feminist effort targeting the infrastructure of music consumption. Research

---

[1] https://smirnoff.withspotify.com/. Launched in early March 2018, the equalizer (from here on I will omit the alcohol company's name) worked for about two years before it was taken down. As I write this in 2021, it seems uncertain if the equalizer is dead, dormant or has reappeared as the EQUAL hub on Spotify. In a previous article, I have focused on the marketing of the tool (Werner 2020a).

on Spotify has shown that female artists are recommended less often (Eriksson & Johansson 2017), how male artists' networks are promoted by Spotify's algorithms (Werner 2020b) and that female artists are streamed very little in most genres except pop (Epps-Darling, Bouyer & Cramer 2020). The inequality in streaming services is affecting female artists' income because streaming revenue is important, especially during the years of the pandemic when live venues have been closed. Thus, it is not only a question of representation, but also the economic and social consequences for artists.

In this chapter, the focus shifts from artists and their feminist work within the music industries, which was the focus of Chapters 1 and 2. The aim in this chapter is to discuss the equalizer's potential, a software intervention for gender equality, and to map the gendered representations in artists' songs among the most-streamed songs on the music streaming service Spotify in 2019. The equalizer is contextualized by three other efforts to promote equality and diversity by music streaming services: Apple Music's #GlobalFeminism, Tidal's *Path to Pride* and Black Lives Matter (BLM) playlists on Spotify, Apple Music and Tidal. Music streaming services are instrumental for artists to make money from their music. Spotify is the music streaming service with the most paying subscribers in the world – 172 million in the third quarter of 2021. Spotify is also agenda setting with its software solutions and business model, and depends on record labels for music content, investors and advertising for capital (Prey 2020). What artists are streamed on the service is a question not only of visibility and marketing but also the livelihood of the artists (Marshall 2015). To understand the context of gender equality, queer-inclusive and anti-racist efforts by music streaming services discussed in this chapter, it is crucial to also investigate the music streaming landscapes as such. To answer the second aim, the content of Spotify's top 50 most-streamed songs of the week in four countries (the United States, Mexico, the United Kingdom and Sweden), from January to August 2019, is analysed in the second part of the chapter. The discussion about the most-streamed weekly songs' representation of gender contextualizes the analysis of equality efforts by music streaming services. Using these two different materials, the equalizer and the most-streamed songs, the chapter discusses both the gender equality efforts of music streaming services and the representations of gender on Spotify, concluding that while the gender equality efforts branded the streaming service as 'good', the dominance of male artists continued in 2019. However, diverse representations of gender do exist among the most-streamed artists, a Black queer rapper (Lil Nas X) and a feminist teenager promoting body positivity (Billie Eilish) stand out as two of the most successful artists. Only looking at the numbers, and not examining qualitatively the types of masculinities and femininities gaining streams, is shown to be insufficient.

Algorithmic culture and feminist algorithm studies

Framing the discussions of gender equality and representations of gender in music streaming in this chapter are previous scholarly discussions on algorithmic culture and feminist studies of algorithms. Both fields of research approach the relation of technology to culture as processual, where technology and culture interact in shaping what music listening is. From this perspective, the software architecture of a music streaming service is not a channel for music to travel through, but an agent shaping what music is today. Using this theoretical understanding of streaming, the 'numbers' on Spotify are not representing real people's taste patterns. Rather, the most-streamed songs and the songs recommended by the equalizer are representations that *claim* to mirror the activity of real listeners while it is also shaped by software activity on the service, through recommendation algorithms, the streaming service's interface and other unknown factors in the structure of the service.

Algorithmic software builds the visual interface of music streaming services as well as everything from the content in recommendations given to listeners, to the order of songs on software-curated playlists (Bonini & Gandini 2019) and when, how and what banners are shown. The infrastructure of music streaming is a result of the work of underlying algorithms, and the algorithmic work is never completed because the infrastructure of Spotify, Apple Music and Tidal is constantly changing. The introduction of algorithms into the mediation of cultural practices, like gaming, music listening or film and television watching, has been understood as 'algorithmic culture' (Galloway 2006). Ted Striphas (2015: 396) has defined algorithmic culture as that which occurs when computational processes do cultural work: the sorting, classifying and hierarchization of people, places, objects and ideas. The term has been used by scholars aiming to understand, for example, how streaming services like Netflix (Hallinan & Striphas 2016) are changing the cultural practices of consumption when software technology, algorithms, cultural commodities and movies interact in the recommendation, production and marketing of content. Spotify and other music streaming services are building their capitalist business models on big data utilized by algorithms to present and recommend music to the listener in an organized manner (Eriksson et al. 2019, Johansson et al. 2017). Recommendations to listeners (Eriksson & Johansson 2017, Werner 2020b) and curated playlists are at the core of how music streaming services operate algorithmically (Bonini & Gandini 2019, Prey 2020) and the services are examples of the sorting, classifying and hierarchization of people and objects done by algorithms that Striphas (2015) discusses. While the services in algorithmic culture often present searches or recommendations either as personalized and 'recommended for you' or as based on 'crowd wisdom' (Striphas 2015: 407), mirroring the popular choices among all people in the world, or in a country, on for example, top lists, the programmed parameters of the software are trade secrets and their decisive power for the cultural outcome is hidden. Also, the services' position as systems of power outside the streaming services themselves is multilayered and in need of investigation (Beer 2017). Striphas (2015) argues that companies selling culture algorithmically are the new intermediaries of culture, and that their selection processes are largely unaccounted for.

In an adjoining discussion, feminist scholars have analysed how algorithms construct ideas and representations of gender and race. In her studies of the Google search engine, Safiya Noble (2018) has concluded that typing 'Black girls' into the search engine results in heavily racialized and sexualized descriptions, images and news, with overt racism, pornography and prejudice in the top results (Noble 2018: 98). The search results portray racialized pornification of young female Black bodies as well as stereotypical images of 'the angry black woman' and 'jezebels' (ibid.), furthering racism and sexism. Noble's studies of the Google search engine highlight how racism and sexism can be the result when commodities and ideas are sorted and presented by algorithms. As she argues: there is no neutrality or accountability in how Google's searches are presented and ordered. Further, Rena Bivens (2017) has investigated how Facebook's code is dependent on a gender-binary definition of humans despite the interface giving multiple options for gender identification, and even though the options have changed over time, the gender binary is at the heart of how Facebook orders people and subsequently markets commodities to them. Gendering in targeted advertisements is one visible result of the gender binary on Facebook. Giving another example of how algorithmic choices construct group identities and sort people, Sophie Bishop (2018) has studied the interplay between algorithmically created genres and middle-class gender expressions in YouTube beauty vloggers. Bishop argues that algorithmically driven commercial choices result in white, middle-class, feminine vloggers being on top in YouTube recommendations and searches. Together with Noble and Bivens, her research findings strongly indicate that algorithmic culture is sorting, classifying and hierarchizing gender, race and class while sorting, classifying and hierarchizing cultural content across streaming services, search engines and social media. That such gendering is also present in the algorithmic recommendations systems of Spotify has been shown quantitatively (Eriksson & Johansson 2017) and qualitatively (Werner 2020b). And possibly this has been noticed by Spotify themselves, since they proceeded to promote gender equality in 2018.

Equalizing music streaming services

In 2018 and 2019, several music streaming platforms provided listeners with playlists, videos and tools to promote female artists, artists outside of the heterosexual or gender-binary norm and feminism in general.[2] In

---

[2] In this chapter, the terminology 'female' and 'male' artists is used to describe artists who are gendered as 'women' and 'men' and called 'she' and 'he' by Spotify, and by themselves in self-presentations on various social media. Artists outside of the gender binary in the material were few (Sam Smith, a non-binary artist, and LP, a gender-neutral artist, were the only two in the material from the most-streamed lists of Spotify; Dorian Electra, a gender-fluid artist, was part of Tidal's Pride Twitter videos in 2019). Artists not identifying as male or female are addressed in line with their gender identity and pronouns when discussed. Gender is not a fixed entity and not given prior to the representations in music. It is therefore important to note that the artists discussed here may identify and be represented differently years after the chapter was written.

2020, the streaming services stood in solidarity with Black Lives Matter, denouncing racism and promoting playlists representing Black artists. These interventions are seen here as responses to social inequalities in the world, *and* to the skewed balance of songs streamed where male artists presenting as heterosexual and cis-normative dominate (Epps-Darling, Bouyer & Cramer 2020). Not excluding this perspective, the interventions are also understood as marketing efforts by companies using social consciousness as a product branding strategy to please their audiences. Feminism, lesbian, gay, bisexual, transgender, queer and others (LGBTQ+) solidarity and anti-racism can be employed by commercial companies as proof of being 'good' or 'with the times', and such good values are used to strengthen a brand and sell goods (Murray 2013, Sobande 2021).

Promoting gender equality by using the equalizer made sense to target young audiences in a competitive business market for music streaming services in the late 2010s when gender and sexuality was a hot topic after #MeToo and other feminist social media campaigns discussed in Chapter 2.[3] Among the music streaming services in 2021, Spotify holds the largest share of the subscription market followed by Apple Music, Amazon and Tencent (exclusively for the Chinese market), and has been in first place for many years.[4] The equalizer as a tool was therefore potentially equalizing the listening to 'men and women artists' on the largest (subscription) music streaming service in the world. The equalizer's software depended on a gender binary since the tool coded two types of artists: male and female. After the equalizer had analysed a listener's account (what data it analysed and from what period were not disclosed), you were encouraged to adjust the percentage of female artists on a playlist, presented visually with a pitch slider from a DJ mixer. You could move the

---

[3] Marketing themselves as 'agents of change' is not Spotify's only strategy. Spotify attracted media debate in 2020 by acquiring podcasts by Joe Rogan, famously associated with the US alt-right. In January 2022, Neil Young and Joni Mitchell announced they wanted their music taken off Spotify due to medical disinformation on the Joe Rogan podcast. Spotify chose to keep Joe Rogan during the last days of January 2022. The company's political alliances appear to be motivated by profit.

[4] https://www.statista.com/statistics/653926/music-streaming-service-subscriber-share/ (accessed 21 January 2022).

slider up and down and change the percentage of female/male artists on the suggested playlist. Looking at the playlists produced by the equalizer, the coding of songs as either female or male used data from Spotify's library of biographies when artists were defined as he/male and she/female. Thus, no gender-mixed groups or artists defining themselves outside the gender binary could be included in the data. Songs had to be 'F' or 'M', promoting the idea that gender is binary and stable. But a song credited to, for example, Lady Gaga could appear as female even if it featured a male co-artist. If that song had been credited to Lady Gaga alone it was understood as female by the equalizer algorithm. The equalizer drew on data from Spotify, then divided the said data into two groups and organized it into playlists for equalizing purposes. The equalizer was making decisions about the way information was presented and organized and what was indicated as important (Bucher 2018: 34). Taina Bucher (2018) argues that this indication of what is important is where the power of algorithms lies. The algorithm has the power to highlight some things for the listener and hide others. When the listener was encouraged to adjust the percentage of 'women artists' on the playlist recommended by the equalizer, most of the choices had already been made by the software, deciding who was female and what songs were in the pool of songs drawn on for the playlist a listener received. The equalizer, an algorithmic tool, was also indicating this adjustment (to increase listening to female artists) as important, rendering the pool of songs presented on the playlists less important.

In the marketing video for the equalizer, Tim Ganss, head of music intelligence, refers to 2017 when all the top 10 most-streamed songs on Spotify were performed by male artists.[5] Ganss argues that this does not represent the good work done by female artists in 2017, motivating the equalizer. The autumn of 2017 saw the breakthrough of the worldwide #MeToo movement, which concerned the music industries. Later, the documentary series *Surviving R Kelly* (2019) about the artist R Kelly's sexual conduct with minors aired.

---

[5] Watch the video here: https://www.youtube.com/watch?v=J__e9LwX5T8 (accessed 6 September 2021).

Russell Simmons, founder of the record company Def Jam, left the United States for Bali in 2017 amid rape allegations from multiple women, later depicted in the documentary *On the Record* (2020). The equalizer was timely, released when gender equality and sexual violence in the music industries were being debated.

The equalizer did not tell you that 50/50 was the ideal, you could decide for yourself what percentage of female artists you wanted on your equalized playlist. Still, the presentation of the task implied that you needed to adjust your listening with an increased number of female, rather than male, artists since the equalizer told you to 'Discover more amazing music by moving the slider to increase the number of women artists in your personalized playlist'. The habit of making women the problem and the object of gender equality efforts has been discussed widely in feminist scholarship (cf Squires 2005, Prügl 2011). In one such critique, Sara Ahmed has argued that making the group in need of being included, in her work gendered and racialized others, an object of the efforts for inclusion risks emphasizing ideas about their subordination and difference (Ahmed 2012). This strategy of singling out the other as the object and the problem of gender equality is performed by the equalizer. This idea, making female artists the object of equality efforts, is mirrored in 2022 by the genre and campaign EQUAL – launched in March 2021 – on Spotify. The genre is not really a musical genre but a hub, a container for thirty-five playlists with female artists from many countries and genres motivating the listener to 'listen to women from the whole world, at full volume', the flagship playlist is EQUAL global. Like the equalizer, EQUAL makes equality an issue about women, and when women are the problem of equality (no matter how great they are) this risks stereotyping them.

When the equalizer was debated online, the tool's choices of known female solo artists like Ariana Grande and Cardi B on equalized playlists were questioned. Why not recommend female artists challenging gender norms, or unknown artists, instead of sticking with 'safe options'?[6] The reason may

---

[6] https://albumchats.wordpress.com/2018/03/18/smirnoff-equalizer-solving-equality-or-virtue-signalling/ (accessed 6 September 2021).

have been that the equalizer algorithm was not designed to bring up unknown artists or identify artists who are feminist or trendy. It was constructed to suggest increasing listening to female artists who already have a lot of streams, artists in the genres to whom the listener had already listened. Since the recommendation algorithms leaned heavily towards male artists (Eriksson & Johansson 2017), the pool of much-streamed female artists was small, making the recommendations that the equalizer gave the listener imprecise. The sorting, classifying and hierarchization of female artists and their songs on the equalized playlists thus resulted in presenting female artists *as* mainstream artists. While claiming to promote women artists, it promoted much-streamed women artists often resulting in mainstream acts being recommended. The representation of female artists as mainstream does something in terms of gender representation, since the mainstream of pop music is often perceived as uninteresting, shallow and unimportant popular music by music journalists and fans (Baker et al. 2013). The equalizer algorithm is hiding less famous female artists and by doing so may give the impression that there are no new/unknown female artists for the listener to discover. The crowd logic used by the algorithm thus fails to correspond to its goal to provide more discovery, exposure and opportunity for great female artists.[7]

Researching the equalizer as a gender equality effort by software, I realized that other streaming services were also promoting gender equality, LGBTQ+ inclusivity, diversity and feminism.[8] Another of the biggest music streaming services, Apple Music, released their film, playlist and hashtag #GlobalFeminism with Annie Lennox and NGO The Circle the day before International Women's Day in 2019.[9] The video addresses issues of gender equality in the world, not gender equality in the music industries, by challenging gender inequality broadly, in all countries and all aspects of life. Similar to the equalizer, gender is constructed as binary (men/women); however, the goal of gender equality

---

[7] https://www.youtube.com/watch?v=WXqZt6nC1VQ (accessed 6 September 2021).
[8] An anonymous reviewer of my article on the marketing of the equalizer (Werner 2020a) helped me see this. Thank you!
[9] The release dates of the efforts, around 8 March, Pride month or Black Lives Matter protests signal (ironically) that the interest in equality may not be present all year around.

work is described in several ways. Notably, the playlist GlobalFeminism on Apple Music features songs performed by female artists. They have been selected as songs by 'visionary female artists' and the results include solo artists like Aretha Franklin, Alanis Morrissette, Nina Simone and Dolly Parton and three gender-mixed groups among twenty-two songs.[10] Another example of a diversity effort by a music streaming service, not focusing on 'women' but on gender identity and sexuality, was released by Tidal in June 2018. The docuseries titled *Path to Pride* aimed to 'elevate some of the most inspiring LGBTQ+ artists today'.[11] In three episodes, the artists Mary Lambert, Alice Bag and Serpentwithfeet discuss gender identity and sexuality in their personal lives as well as their music and career. Tidal continued to celebrate LGBTQ+ artists on Twitter during US pride month in 2019 with videos featuring personal messages from artists about how they relate their gender identity and sexuality in music. Tove Lo, Carlos Vara, iLoveMakonnen, Dorian Electra and several others were featured on the Tidal Twitter account and the hashtag used was #PRIDE.[12] The motivation for including the efforts by Apple Music and Tidal here is that, like the equalizer, they both address gender equality or gender and sexuality with the aim to make the world more equal. Marketing themselves as agents of social change, for women, feminism and inclusivity for all gender identities and sexualities, the music streaming services Spotify, Apple Music and Tidal all project images of themselves as 'good'.

Returning to the equalizer, an algorithm to numerically equalize music listening between male and female artists, Spotify has not only marketed an equalizing project but also proposed to change listening patterns with an equality algorithm that intervenes with musical practice, rather than talks about equality, and this distinguishes the equalizer from the other socially conscious marketing examples. That there is plenty of inequality in how data and algorithms function has been shown by, for example, Noble's (2018)

---

[10] https://music.apple.com/us/playlist/globalfeminism/pl.95129d7ed1c1481fa6b6071b0f86a029 (accessed 6 September 2021).

[11] https://tidal.com/magazine/article/path-to-pride-serpentwithfeet-and-devin-morris/1-51346 (accessed 6 September 2021).

[12] https://twitter.com/tidal/status/1139589727030583299 (accessed 6 September 2021).

research on the Google search engine. The pool of data used, the way it is used and for what goals must be problematized since data is often used for power (D'Ignazio & Klein 2020: 12). In 2020, the ethical aspects of automatic computational processes, machine learning and artificial intelligence (AI) were discussed in relation to Google's firing of Timnit Gebru. She was fired over a paper that Google claimed had not been reviewed and submitted properly. Gebru, a known advocate for Black people in AI, and a particular critic of facial recognition software was assigned to develop Google's ethics in software. While the debates about commercial interests' relation to critical research is beyond the scope of this chapter, Smirnoff and Spotify did attempt to create an algorithm that challenged what they saw as bias (male artists dominating the streams) at a time when algorithms were being problematized as sexist and racist. Still, there are many ways of envisioning what gender equality and social justice are and how to achieve them. What kind of gender equality did the equalizer advance?

Judith Squires (2005) has argued that gender mainstreaming policies, the most common method for gender equality work in the political sphere, can be divided into three types: integrating, agenda setting and transformative gender mainstreaming.[13] Integrating gender mainstreaming employs experts who, by technocratic means, even out the numbers of men/women in organizations; agenda-setting gender mainstreaming collaborates with interest groups to identify problems of discrimination within organizations; and transformative gender mainstreaming aims to transform the everyday practices and policies of organizations that have discriminatory effects.[14] Squires (2005: 374) argues that integrating gender mainstreaming can be very successful: the goals of levelling out the numbers of men/women are easy to grasp and are often presented as 'good for all', for the organization or business. The equalizer was an integrating gender equality effort since it focused on the numbers of

---

[13] For a definition of gender mainstreaming, see the Introduction of the book.
[14] Gender mainstreaming has been integrated policy in the European Union for decades, and the ideas have spread to businesses such as the music industries. Even if the creative industries have been shown to be resistant to 'bureaucratic' governance, programmes like Creative Europe fund the arts and implement gender mainstreaming. Creative Europe and gender mainstreaming in the music industries will be further addressed in Chapter 4.

men and women and employed the technocratic methods of a website and an algorithm created by experts. The integrating strategy also risks what Squires calls rhetoric entrapment when gender equality is presented as increasing the quality of an organization. If the results of the policy do not deliver improved quality, the whole effort may be perceived as a failure and gender equality work is abandoned. The equalizer was driven by quality arguments, listening to great female artists, and failed to deliver playlists with artists unknown or loved by the listener. The equalizer's efforts of gender equality in music streaming were subsequently abandoned by Smirnoff and Spotify. It seems that the equalizer was the victim of the risks of integrating gender mainstreaming as pointed out by Squires (2005). It failed to deliver the great music and playlists by women it promised to listeners.[15]

Further, the equalizer was placed outside Spotify's recommendation algorithms that manage the music streaming service, it was even on a separate site. To transform with gender mainstreaming, Squires (2005) argues, the inner functioning of an organization and practice must be addressed and transformed. Squires argues that the practice of transformative gender mainstreaming has the most feminist political potential to achieve social change through equality work in organizations.

The way Spotify sorted and presented music on the music streaming service was not affected by the equalizer, and the algorithmic culture of Spotify was not altered. Bucher (2018: 20) argues that algorithms are computational processes that can be very different depending on what data is fed to them and how the choices the algorithms make are programmed. Algorithmic culture is not destined to enforce sexism and racism or support neoliberal capitalism. Algorithms can be disruptive to power systems. Thus, 'gender' could at least theoretically be programmed into the main algorithms of the Spotify service. The listener could, for example, set their default to 50 per cent female artists for all recommendations made in 'discover weekly', a function that recommends new music personalized for the listener. While that gender

---

[15] As pointed out before, the equalizer seems to have been translated into EQUAL, a hub or genre on Spotify since March 2021. This effort by Spotify is yet to be researched.

mainstreaming effort would hold more potential for promoting female artists, it would not bring about gender equality. Elizabeth Prügl (2011) has discussed the employment of diversity management and gender mainstreaming as governmentality, using Michel Foucault's definition of the concept, and argued that feminism is normalized into governmental rationales by the popularization of gender mainstreaming. Feminist knowledge has become part of neoliberal governing. While she states that feminist knowledge has changed governmental practice, she also argues that the integration of feminist knowledge through gender mainstreaming has changed the feminist goal by depoliticizing it. Because gender equality in the music industries cannot be deflated to the number of streamed songs by female artists, the feminist critique of the music industries loses its edge in numerically focused efforts like the equalizer.

The idea of integrating the equalizer into every Spotify recommendation highlights how gender equality is placed outside the algorithmic culture; however, even if it were inside Spotify its potential would be limited. To strive for change, Prügl (2011: 86) suggests two routes: disruption or reflection. Disruption through challenging taboos, prohibitions and inhibitions, and reflection by continuously advancing methods for feminist struggles to ensure awareness of effects, and counter processes that normalize feminism into governing rationales. The equalizer's focus on the integration of female artists could never challenge sexism in lyrics and videos, the interplay with ageism and racism facing female artists or male networks within the music industries. Neither does it show an interest in evolving feminist methods, counting women and men is a well-known approach to gender and power, rhetorically strong but with limited effects.

The equalizer's spokesperson in 2018 was Honey Dijon, a DJ, a Black transwoman from Chicago now residing in New York. She is known as an activist for trans rights and inclusion in electronic dance music. Dijon's selection as the face of the equalizer may indicate that trans rights and anti-racism were also on the table, besides listening equality between male and female artists. However, inequalities other than those based on binary gender division are not significant for how the equalizer functioned. The focus of the debate in early 2018 was on gender equality and sexual violence, but the spring of 2020 saw a pandemic, and the killing of African-American George Floyd and Breonna Taylor (among others) by police was followed by US nationwide protests from, or associated with, the Black Lives Matter (BLM) movement. Tidal was reported to have donated 1.5 million dollars to BLM in 2020 and Tidal, Spotify and Apple Music all edited playlists called Black Lives Matter. The subtitle on Tidal was 'anthems of change/songs for motivation', on Spotify it was 'ALL black lives matter. Songs of empowerment and pride', while Apple Music wrote 'a collection across decades of songs empowering the movement'. Tidal's subtitle focused on political and social change and the motivation needed to reach it; Spotify's subtitle focused on (Black) group identity as a source of pride and empowerment; and Apple Music highlighted the social movement as an object of empowerment through music. The content of the Tidal and Apple Music playlists were US-based Black artists, while Spotify's list also featured Black artists from other countries.[16] Spotify linked the BLM playlist to the US-based NGO Color of Change, writing 'take action on racial justice, visit Color of Change'. The NGO is a partner of Black Lives Matter founded in 2005 after Hurricane Katrina and focuses on racial justice and civil rights in the United States. Given the heated debate about BLM in the United States, this signals that Spotify is supporting racial justice, but not BLM, while Tidal openly supported BLM. Compared to the equalizer's sorting of female artists by gender, popularity and genre, BLM playlists highlight the separation of gender from race on music streaming services: male artists are dominating all three lists. The equalizer does not consider gender equality and racism together nor are they both considered on BLM playlists. That the consideration of sexism and racism together is possible in music was demonstrated by the #MuteRKelly campaign (founded in the summer of 2017, before #MeToo exploded) where race, class, age and gender were clearly invoked in a critical analysis of artist R Kelly and the disappearance of young Black girls, often from poor families. The goal of this movement, to mute and prosecute the artist, was individually targeting one person. Again, displaying a

---

[16] These discussions mirror the playlists as they looked in December 2020. Playlists are, of course, subject to change.

logic where the individual becomes the problem rather than the structure that supports the abuse of power. Consideration of the power imbalances based on several sociocultural categories interacting made the campaign against R Kelly effective, revealing several types of oppressions in the music industries. Still, the goal – to put R Kelly in jail – does not affect the music industries as a whole.

Drawing on the analysis so far, it seems unlikely that music streaming services by themselves can achieve the goals of their equality and diversity rhetoric. Seeing the equalizer, *Path to Pride*, Global Feminism and BLM playlists as marketing, where feminism, gay-friendliness and anti-racism are commodified (Goldman 1992) to make the companies appear to be 'agents of change' rather than profit seekers is hard to avoid. Fransesca Sobande (2021: 142) has argued that BLM is included in marketing discourses in ways that she considers anti-Black, rather than anti-racist. The marketability of feminism and strong women has already been discussed as a post-feminist market logic in Chapter 1. Despite the flaws of the gender mainstreaming work of the equalizer, and despite the commodification of feminism, LGBTQ+ friendliness and anti-racism in all the discussed efforts, I wanted to take a closer look at the possible achievements of the equalizer. When the equalizer was marketed in 2019, Smirnoff and Spotify claimed that female artists had become more listened to because of the equalizer.[17] It was claimed that there had been a 52 per cent increase in women artists streamed through Spotify. It was also stated that the balance was 70/30 between men and women artists in streaming on Spotify. It was very unclear how the numbers presented had been generated, for example how gender-mixed groups or non-binary artists were counted, what time the numbers had been collected, what regions, what genres and so on. I was curious about the numerical representation of gender on Spotify as well as what artists were the most streamed and how they appeared gendered musically and visually. How many songs performed by female artists made it on to the Spotify top lists after the equalizer? And what gender representations were considered as popular by the algorithms of Spotify?

---

[17] https://www.youtube.com/watch?v=WXqZt6nC1VQ (accessed 6 September 2021).

Analysing gender in the most-streamed songs on Spotify 2019

To get an idea of the algorithmic construction of 'most streamed' in relation to quantitative and qualitative gender representation, I mapped the top 50 most-streamed songs in Mexico, the United Kingdom, the United States and Sweden between the first and thirty-second week of 2019.[18] The lists I analysed were 'Spotify weekly top 200' in each country. These lists are compiled once a week with 200 songs. I mapped the top 50 of the weekly top 200 in four countries and compared the analysis with the list of the top 50 most-streamed songs on Spotify internationally for all of 2019, as presented by Spotify. Spotify's largest markets are in Europe and America and that is the motivation for the selected countries. I wanted to include China or South Korea, as well as Nigeria or South Africa, since these are big music markets outside of Europe and America. But there was no (or in the case of South Africa very little) data available because Spotify is not established in those countries.

The discussion of gender representation on the most-streamed lists is aimed at contextualizing the efforts for gender equality and diversity by music streaming services. It simultaneously contributes with an analysis of what amounts and types of gendered representations are created by the algorithmic culture of streaming services' top lists. The gendering is both quantitative, how many female, male, non-binary and gender-neutral artists, as well as mixed groups, are presented to be in the top lists, and qualitative, what types

---

[18] I downloaded the data from Academic Rights Press archive Music Industry Data (Music ID) (https://www.academicrightspress.com/entertainment/music (accessed 8 February 2021)). The weekly top 200 lists from Spotify were almost always incomplete. Up to eleven songs were missing and few lists included all top 50 songs. A spokesperson for Music ID explained that data gets lost in the transfer from Spotify. It was also common that one of several artists was the only one connected to a particular song, therefore all songs had to be carefully listened to (and watched on YouTube) by the author to find out what artists were performing them: 5,627 songs were coded (1,375 from the United States, 1,388 from the United Kingdom, 1,409 from Mexico and 1,455 from Sweden), though some songs appeared many times in the material and they were counted every time. They give a varied image of gendered representation on Spotify's most-streamed lists. There is no indication that the missing songs would have changed the larger picture of gender representation when coding so many songs. All songs were listened to, the videos (if there was a video) were watched and the artists' bios were read on Spotify and Wikipedia.

of femininities, masculinities and other genders are constructed as being in the top lists. As discussed, lists on Spotify are understood as an interface constructed by the algorithmic culture of the service: sorting, classifying and hierarchizing music. The lists are presented as composed of the songs that are the most popular to stream in one country during the previous week, in the order of popularity. Two things are important to keep in mind though: popular means streamed the most times and the recommendation algorithm also promotes the most-streamed songs to listeners, giving them more streams.

One stream is the singular data that together with other streams makes up the 18,516,701 streams of Billie Eilish's song 'Bad Guy' during the week leading up to 4 April 2019 in the United States. The song was released on 29 March and between that day and 4 April it received 18.5 million streams on Spotify in the United States, according to my material. To be counted as a stream, a song must be played for thirty seconds or more. There is no guarantee that a person is listening. In 2019, a discussion about how the music streaming revenue business model was tricked by troll farms selling 'fake streams' featured in the media, and Spotify teamed up with other companies to combat the practice.[19] The idea behind fake streams is to buy streams of a particular song from a troll farm where employees programme bots to stream a song a certain number of times for money. According to the debate, the rationale is to get the song noticed by algorithms on the music streaming service and generate recommendations, inclusion in playlists followed by 'real streams'. The practice of fake streams and the shadow economy of troll farms work (Drott 2020) because Spotify's algorithms promote already popular songs (Eriksson et al. 2019). If one can make a song seem popular, recommendation algorithms will promote it. Using a perspective where technology and cultural practices interact, 'fake streams' would therefore not be outside of the algorithmic logic, but a performance of it. This performance challenges Spotify's control over their revenue since other agents make money. Fake streams are a challenge to the business model of global big tech companies where a loophole in the system is used and

---

[19] https://www.ft.com/content/371b7b96-92e1-11e9-aea1-2b1d33ac3271 (accessed 6 September 2021).

cheap labour is exploited (Drott 2020). Glitches and technological failure are part of how technology works (Sundén 2016). The functions of technology and software systems are often idealised, yet sometimes they do not function in the exact way imagined. Such technological failure has been theorized by Jenny Sundén (2016) as potential sites of political disruption. In her work, the gender binary is disrupted, and the fake streams could challenge the neoliberal capitalist system of big tech. Troll farms also have monetary gain in sight and from a world system perspective they are not placed outside of capitalism. But if they do not do it for the money, are they fake streaming artists with the aim of disrupting power? They could be an example of Prügl's (2011) proposal to disrupt power through challenging taboos, prohibitions and inhibitions, and troll farms could be used as a method for furthering feminist aims.

To historically situate the discussion about fake streams, it is also crucial to remember that in the past there have been payouts to radio stations for playing records, and practices of buying a particular record in bulk to advance it on top lists. Payola is a socio-economic practice aimed at bringing about the inclusion of a material, like a song, in a broadcasted programme (Coase 1979) and has long been a practice in radio despite it being initially seen as unethical and later made illegal. In 2020, a new feature on Spotify was described as a form of payola and discussed in the media. By letting Spotify have a cut of their royalties, artists could give their songs an 'algorithmic boost' and get featured more on playlists.[20] Essentially, the artist is paying Spotify for a similar favour that other artists have (allegedly) purchased from troll farms. A final example of how the algorithmic culture of Spotify interplays with capitalism is the targeted pop-up visual advertisements used to promote new songs by Spotify, in collaboration with artists and record companies. The pop-ups are bought by labels or artists for a small sum every time a listener clicks on them to listen to the song that is being advertised.[21] It is obvious from these examples that all songs are not treated the same by the Spotify algorithms. Therefore, it makes

---

[20] https://www.theguardian.com/technology/2020/nov/03/spotify-artists-promote-music-exchange-cut-royalty-rates-payola-algorithm (accessed 6 September 2021).
[21] https://www.musicbusinessworldwide.com/spotify-marquee-ads-cost-55-cents-per-click-advises-spend-of-at-least-5k-report/ (accessed 6 September 2021).

sense to understand the most-streamed lists as constructions where software is interplaying with human actions. The most-streamed lists are a performance of the sum of these processes. The lists analysed here are also affected by the software of MusicID, the source of my material, where some songs were lost, and some data therefore excluded.

Now, turning to the material, the overall image of the quantitative representation of gendered artists on Spotify top lists in the four countries was that male artists dominated the lists:[22] 77 per cent of the streamed songs were performed by male artists in the United States, 76 per cent of the songs were performed by male artists in Mexico, 63 per cent in Sweden and 66 per cent in the United Kingdom.[23] Looking at female artists, 15 per cent of the songs on the US most-streamed lists were performed by female artists, 7 per cent of the songs on the lists in Mexico were performed by female artists, 22 per cent in Sweden and 19 per cent in the United Kingdom. Songs performed by several artists of mixed genders accounted for 7 per cent of the songs on the US top lists, 16 per cent of the songs on the Mexico top lists, 14 per cent in Sweden and 15 per cent in the United Kingdom. Only two artists were defined outside of the gender binary on the lists analysed: Sam Smith (non-binary) and LP (gender-neutral), who accounted for 0.2–1 per cent of the songs in the four countries, a very small but significant proportion of the lists. Significant because visibility for artists outside of the gender binary is low in the music industries. A study in which Spotify researchers were co-authors found comparable numbers in worldwide streaming with one in five streams associated with a female or multi-gender group (Epps-Darling, Bouyer & Cramer 2020: 250).[24] The US top lists stand out by representing few songs performed by groups

---

[22] When coding the material, I used four categories: female artists, male artists, non-binary or other genders and groups with mixed genders. All songs were listened to and watched on YouTube and artists' pages on Wikipedia and biographies on Spotify were used to determine the gendered presentation of artists as 'he', 'she' or 'they'. This was necessary since the data collected from MusicID was often incomplete, it did not list all performers of the songs. If there was more than one artist on a song but they were all women, the song was coded as performed by a female artist, vice versa with songs featuring more than one male artist. How many artists were on a song was not coded, only gender was quantitatively recorded.

[23] Every song entering the charts was counted every time it appeared. If the same song was on the charts twice in the same week in two different remixes it was counted twice.

[24] This study does not account for genders outside of male/female.

or collaborating artists with mixed genders. Any song featuring artists who were both female, male, non-binary or gender-neutral was counted as mixed. A song like 'South of the Border' that would be credited to Ed Sheeran when it comes to paying out royalties was coded as mixed because it features Cardi B and Camila Cabello. While I would argue that numbers in themselves do not say much about gender equality in the music industries as a whole – they are representations of gender on algorithmically constructed playlists – Smirnoff and Spotify themselves claimed in 2019 that the equalizer had advanced numerical gender equality. While this may be true for the unknown sample they analysed, the most-streamed songs in my sample were heavily dominated by male artists, and female artists did not reach 30 per cent in any of the four countries.

Looking more closely at the kinds of masculinities that were dominating the charts in a qualitative analysis of the top lists in all four countries, there was a notable presence of Black, brown and othered masculinities performing genres like rap, hip hop and reggaeton (or Latin trap). These artists often promoted a muscular, gun-carrying, dangerous or 'thug' sort of masculinity, surrounding themselves with young women wearing revealing clothes in the videos. At the same time, some of the most popular male artists were white men, like Ed Sheeran and Post Malone. Two types of masculinities can be contrasted using the representations of masculinity in the music videos for Bad Bunny featuring Drake 'Mia' and Ed Sheeran featuring Camila Cabello and Cardi B 'South of the Border', both popular songs in the material. In the first video, Bad Bunny and Drake are hosting a block party where most of the guests are young and beautiful women in hotpants and tops showing cleavage. There's a barbeque, the (few) men at the party are gambling at a table and the artists are rapping with a car or a sound system behind them. Bad Bunny and Drake wear loose-fitting clothes and gold chains, and use their arms to make large gestures, imitating holding a gun for example. The house in the background is a small one level, as often featured in US films depicting poor inner-city areas in Los Angeles or Miami. Smoking, drinking out of paper cups and booty dancing appear in the video, representing ideas about Black and brown masculinities as tough, drinking, car loving, poor and girl crazy. Like 'Mia', 'South of the Border' is a song about love. Ed Sheeran is introduced in a castle described as outside of London in text appearing on-screen, singing to a well-heeled and well-dressed crowd in a tuxedo. The video is introduced as a 'spy film' and clearly plays with typical scenes from James Bond movies, for example Ed Sheeran is drugged while drinking scotch from a thick glass at a bar in the castle and is abducted by a woman in a red dress. Later, he is alone in a control room, still in his tuxedo but without the jacket, overlooking monitors, walkie-talkie in hand. Where 'Mia' plays on racist ideas of Black and brown men in the United States, 'South of the Border' plays with the James Bond figure of white British masculinity, polite, smart, strong, dangerous and in control, essentially 'good'. Both videos hold ironic potential, but for the purposes of analysis here the masculinities portrayed are seen as both hegemonic – both of them popular in contemporary music culture – and clearly racialized as Black/brown and white.

Not all Black and brown gangster masculinities were from the United States. 'Drill' artists in the UK were numerous among the most-streamed songs on the UK lists, representing guns, cars and housing estates (and in 'Gun Lean' one female exception to the male dominance: Ms Banks). While the same four gender categories of analysis were applicable over all four countries resulting in most artists being identified as female or male, fewer as gender-mixed groups and a small number as non-binary or gender-neutral, coding ethnicity/race proved more difficult. Racial or ethnic categories of significance varied between all four countries and while debates about racism, racialization and cultural appropriation in music bridged the contexts, these debates were not the same across borders. In Sweden, the racialization of male rappers, where they were described in the media as criminals and dangerous, caused debate during 2019, for example in the case of Greekazo who was othered and racialized in the Swedish media despite him being white with European parents who immigrated from Poland and Greece.[25] Greekazo and other white rappers, Einar (murdered in 2021) for example, were popular on the Swedish most-streamed lists, and rappers in Sweden can be racialized in

---

[25] https://www.svt.se/nyheter/lokalt/stockholm/kritikerstorm-mot-malou-efter-intervju-med-rapparen-greekazo (accessed 9 September 2021).

public discourse in terms of class, ethnicity and/or race without being Black/brown. This makes the racialization of Swedish rappers different from the racialization in the United States where Post Malone, also a white rapper, often featured on the lists with several songs. He has been accused of appropriating African-American culture. In the UK, Ed Sheeran has been accused of appropriating both Irish folk rock and grime (though not at the same time), genres seen as not belonging to him. Appropriation and hybridity in music are present in different genres and times (Born & Hesmondhalgh 2000: 8) and understanding musical appropriation through the lens of race and class should be done in light of a colonial history where racially marginalized groups making little money from their music have seen white artists use non-white musical styles and become successful (ibid.). When artists from racially or ethnically marginalized groups are met with racism and demonization in the media and white artists are celebrated for similar styles in contemporary pop music, described as post-genre (James 2017), this is a sign of racial inequality in music. In debates, the profound racism of this larger issue is often presented as an individual artist doing something bad, stealing music, instead of addressing the larger historical, material and discursive processes that make cultural appropriation beneficial for (mostly) white artists.

Masculinity among most-streamed artists is also complicated when stereotypes, like the Black and brown tough guy, are played with in the psychedelic and ironic music video of Travis Scott featuring Drake 'Sicko mode'. During 2019, Lil Nas X was on the most-streamed lists in all four countries with his song 'Old Town Road' featuring Billy Ray Cyrus (Figure 3.1). Being an openly gay Black man performing a crossover between country music and hip hop in the United States, Lil Nas X became viral and much streamed. He bent the rules of representations in two main ways: first, the country genre is known to be almost exclusively white in the United States; and second, tough, male, Black popular music rappers are strongly associated with heterosexuality and homophobia (Li 2019). In the music video of 'Old Town Road', Lil Nas X rides a horse through a US African-American neighbourhood ending up in a town hall performing with Billy Ray Cyrus and other white musicians while the audience dance a square dance. The music video is a visual game depicting and challenging stereotypes from rap and country music alike. Lil Nas X's hot

Figure 3.1 Lil Nas X eats chicken wings at the 'Old Town Road' premiere party in 2019 wearing one of his outfits from the music video (Getty Images).

pink cowboy outfit, often seen in press photos, functions as a visual sign of queerness. The artist has since moved on to prove that he is no one-hit wonder and homophobia in hip hop has become less accepted in recent years. Rapper DaBaby was, for example, heavily criticized after an incident with homophobic slurs that made the news during a concert in 2021. Homophobic slurs did not previously make headlines in rap concerts.

The racialization and othering of artists who dominate on the most-streamed lists are present in some genres more than others (hip hop, trap, drill, urban, reggaeton, funk carioca, etc.) and those genres also have more Black and brown performers than pop, rock, country or heavy metal. Reading artists' bios on Spotify and Wikipedia, it is striking how national and racial origins are often not mentioned when describing white artists, who might be described with a city or state of birth. But national and racial descriptions are almost always included when describing Black or brown artists. The definitions of who is Black or brown, and the boundaries of Blackness and otherness are not universal, as exemplified by Greekazo. Thus, genres, artists and their performance of race/ethnicity are more difficult to quantify and compare than gender on the most-streamed lists of Spotify. This variety in national contexts also proves race/ethnicity difficult to simplify in an equalizing algorithm.

The most popular songs in 2019 were often reggaeton songs. Looking at the top 50 streamed artists in the world in 2019 as reported by Spotify, there were five male reggaeton artists in the top 12 (Bad Bunny (Puerto Rico), J Balvin (Colombia), Ozuna (Puerto Rico), Daddy Yankee (Puerto Rico) and Anuel AA (Puerto Rico)). In the United States, these artists would be othered as not white, and Puerto Rico and Columbia are both nations with an immigration history to the United States. At the same time, except for Ozuna, the artists are ethnic majority artists in their own contexts, not understanding themselves as Black. The genre, and these artists, were highly present on the lists from the United States and Mexico, but less featured on the lists from the United Kingdom and Sweden. Reggaeton is a genre where a 'Latino' identity is claimed, featuring artists identifying as white, Black and brown held together by the Spanish language and a Latin American culture.

Despite the influence of reggaeton in the United States and Mexico, nation-based artists dominated the charts. Locally produced music was very visible in the top-streamed lists and many artists only appeared on the lists of their country of residence. The use of nation-based IP numbers in Spotify's interface and algorithms can be understood as interplaying with listening patterns and creating visibility for nationally based artists. Spotify recommends the music associated with the national IP address and the music streaming service also routinely sorts genres by nationality, for example Swedish hip hop is separated from French hip hop. The way Spotify defines genre is – the company states – by an algorithm that analyses the sound of the song and the music streaming service categorizes thousands of genres, not only by nation; 'deep melodic hard rock' and 'Swedish idol pop' are both genres on Spotify (Krogh 2020). Thus, French hip hop may not be visible to a listener in Sweden or the United Kingdom on the service unless the listener actively pursues the genre.

When analysing the US top lists, I noticed that several songs by the same artist were often on the same top-streamed list. Ed Sheeran, Billie Eilish, Post Malone and Ariana Grande (the four top-streamed artists in the world in

2019, also white artists from the United States and the United Kingdom) stood out as artists with many songs featured on the lists during the same weeks in all four countries. These songs were all from the same albums. Now, while MTV and Billboard-oriented music consumption patterns focus on the hits and the singles, Spotify and music streaming services in general direct the listener to the page of the artist where the latest album or the whole catalogue can be found, at no extra charge. The software itself and the business model where you pay per month and not per song are therefore shaping top-streamed lists where ten songs by Billie Eilish entered the top 50 streamed list in the United States in the same week. When these songs are top list songs they are promoted further by Spotify by placements on playlists and in recommendations. Also, all the albums by these four white artists were rigorously covered by newspapers, vloggers and in social media marketing, creating an intermedia virality, where Spotify is part of a larger media system embedded in algorithmic culture.

When compared to the representations of masculinities discussed above, female artists displayed little threat or danger to society through violent thug femininities. The most-streamed female artists in all countries were white or white-ish Latina, performing pop or R&B and mostly conforming to beauty standards for young heterosexual females. If we consider the representations of female artists on the most-streamed lists, Billie Eilish and Ariana Grande in particular represented many of the most-streamed songs performed by female artists.[26] Both were also featured on the most-streamed lists in all four countries, and according to Spotify they were number 2 (Billie Eilish) and 3 (Ariana Grande) among the most streamed on Spotify in 2019 worldwide.[27] Billie Eilish (born 2001) and Ariana Grande (born 1993) are also juxtaposed representations of contemporary young femininity. While both are young,

---

[26] Taylor Swift's 'You Need to Calm Down' was streamed a lot, and was noteworthy for its overt support for LGBTQ+ rights in a video featuring known LGBTQ+ profiles (Ellen and Laverne Cox among others). The artist's engagement in the Equality Act was discussed in Chapter 1. Taylor Swift herself did conform with white, young, beauty standard femininity.

[27] Taylor Swift was the next female artist at number 13, followed by Camila Cabello at number 21. Sam Smith was the only non-binary artist at number 24.

Figure 3.2 Billie Eilish speaks onstage at the LACMA Art + Film Gala in 2019 with green highlights in her hair and a loose-fitting Gucci shirt (Getty Images).

white, heterosexual,[28] from the United States and skilled songwriters and singers, their presented femininities vary (Figure 3.2). While Billie Eilish styled her hair in green, grey and blue, at the time, wore oversized sports clothes in her music videos and ironicized about gender stereotypes in 'Bad Guy', Ariana Grande wears her hair in a long high ponytail and dances in tight dresses with high-heeled shoes in her music videos of 'Thank You, Next' and '7 Rings'. Both could also be said to make fun of femininity. Both artists received a lot of media attention in 2019, and Billie Eilish's success could be understood as proof that a female artist who does not promote herself as the bearer of a (hetero) sexy femininity and beauty ideals can succeed. As already

---

[28] Many fans have wished Billie Eilish to be gay. In 2021, her sexuality was up for discussion again. In relation to the music video of 'Lost Cause', it was asked: is she queer or queer baiting? She said that she is heterosexual in 2019. Still, both artists may identify differently later in life in terms of gender identity and sexuality.

discussed in Chapter 1, the success of female artists who defy gender norms of sexy, youthful and heterosexual femininity, or are self-proclaimed feminists, is often seen as an indication of 'progress' for feminist issues in mediated popular music. Zara Larsson, present on the most-streamed lists in Sweden, is a proclaimed feminist. Billie Eilish has been an advocate for body positivity, questioning the norms surrounding female bodies in the music industries. Her breakthrough song 'Bad Guy' ironically presents a toxic masculinity embodied by herself in a music video where she makes fun of the tough, bad guy figure. Still, are the statements and lyrics of Zara Larsson and Billie Eilish more feminist than those of Karol G, Taylor Swift and Ariana Grande? All these artists are supporting women's rights, and statements like these seem a given in contemporary popular music in 2019. What made Billie Eilish stand out in 2019 was her baggy clothes and hair colour, rather than her feminist stance on body positivity. Therefore, gender ideals presented by artists and their stances on feminist or women's politics (and sometimes their sexuality) are often debated together, highlighting the connections between feminism and gender politics.

Returning to the equalizer and the aim of the tool: to equalize music listening between male and female artists, the equalizer had much work to do when 7 per cent of the most-streamed songs in Mexico were performed by female artists in 2019. Sweden's 22 per cent female artists in the top-streamed lists seems a high number and this makes it easier to understand why Smirnoff and Spotify created a tool focusing on visibility for female artists in the first place. The differences in numeric representation are striking, especially in times when many female pop stars have made names for themselves. On the other hand, the context of what is available to stream on Spotify and how many songs on Spotify are performed by female artists is hidden. It can be argued that the pool of data from which algorithms are selecting should be considered before arguing that female artists are under-represented.

The logics of best-of lists as a discursive construct should also be considered. Sorting and hierarchization are at the core of all lists, not only those produced by algorithms: someone is placed first and someone is placed last, coming first is the best result for an artist. Coming first on a Spotify most-streamed list, part of the algorithmic recommendation structure, fake streams, payola, pop-up advertisements and so on is performative, because the placement means that the artist is listened to first by those listeners who are looking for the most popular songs of the moment. That gives the artist more streams and puts them on next week's list. Presenting top lists in the form of playlists is a choice made by the streaming service that is also constructing curated playlists with more room for the most recent releases – not streamed much yet.

The qualitative investigation of most-streamed lists has shown that being a female artist does not mean that one is automatically challenging all sexism in the music industries. The presence of female artists on streaming does not easily translate to gender equality. What then, does it mean to equalize? Transformation and reflection on current practices surrounding the gendering of artists, the representation of artists and popular music itself are necessary to equalize music listening, not just to level out the numbers.

Conclusion

The research that this chapter presents and discusses started when I felt feminist optimism on discovering the equalizer. I believed that this algorithmic tool could be used to transform music streaming's gendered representations and that it was a novel feminist practice in the music industries: a feminist algorithm for gender equality. Algorithmic culture could be revolutionary I thought, not just a neoliberal capitalist logic disguised as crowd wisdom (Striphas 2015). But the more I searched for feminist, LGBTQ+ and anti-racist interventions in music streaming, the less transformative the interventions for gender equality and diversity seemed. While streaming services are marketing themselves as allies, or agents, of social change for women and LGBTQ+ people and as anti-racist, the most-streamed songs on Spotify from 2019 do not indicate social change. Rather, a popular music culture firmly dominated by male artists and divided along the lines of gender and race is presented. Capitalism is at the core of the algorithmic culture and stereotypes are widely employed – whether ironic or not. And the equalizer, together with the interventions of music streaming services discussed in this chapter, appears as a failed gender mainstreaming effort at best. An empty branding strategy at worst.

Turning to the most-streamed lists of Spotify one year after the equalizer was launched, they confirm studies of radio stations and Billboard lists (Crider 2020, Smith et al. 2021) showing a low numerical representation of female, gender-binary and gender-neutral artists. The most-streamed lists hold few female artists, and those who are present are often white, young, slim and sexy. The most-streamed lists also hold many racist visual and lyrical descriptions of Black and brown male artists. While, theoretically, arguments have been made that algorithmic culture (Striphas 2015) and power (Bucher 2018) could result in different outcomes, this study shows that algorithms for music streaming further the success of very few female artists and many more men, and that the females who are succeeding are 'exceptional' in their talent, youth, whiteness and heterosexual address. Making Billie Eilish and Lil Nas X possible exceptions of difference in their gendered representations. While algorithms can gender culture differently, music streaming algorithms studied here favour male artists and female artists with a young desirable femininity. These results indicate tough obstacles for female popular music artists trying to make a living from their music in our supposedly feminist times when streaming services are still increasingly important for the distribution of popular music worldwide.

4

Keychange

Gender equality work in the popular music industries

The last empirical chapter of the book takes a closer look at the feminism expressed and the gender equality work performed by the project Keychange (www.keychange.eu). Keychange was started by PRS Foundation, the UK's leading charitable funder of new music and talent development, together with five other organizations/festivals across Europe. It was launched at the Reeperbahn Festival in 2017, and today Keychange is led by three core partners: Inferno Events/Reeperbahn Festival in Germany, PRS Foundation in the UK and Musikcentrum Öst in Sweden. By 2021, Keychange had music festival partners in twelve countries (eleven in Europe and one in Canada). The ongoing Keychange programme runs from 2019 to 2024. The main objectives of the project are to transform the music industry to a 50:50 gender balance in career development for artists and key persons, a pledge for festivals and other music organizations to achieve gender balance and to promote advocacy for gender balance to national and international policymakers. The core activity of Keychange is to create a network of (female, non-binary, trans) artists and innovators who are supported in their careers through a career development programme ending in the participants performing on the stage of one of the music festival partners.

The expressions used by Keychange to define its goals, like 50:50 and under-represented genders, will be discussed in this chapter with the purpose to analyse and evaluate Keychange's formulations of problems and solutions for gender equality in the music industries. What Keychange constructs as the problem and the solution is investigated through the presented activities, methods, artists and other actions on the Keychange website and the websites of PRS Foundation, Musikcentrum Öst and Reeperbahn Festival. Keychange's gender equality work is framed by previous research on gender equality in the music industries and theories of gender mainstreaming, as discussed in the introduction of the book and Chapter 3. In the conclusion, the potential for Keychange to change the music industries is addressed. The chapter argues firstly that because Keychange has limited time, the project form is a weakness since the work could stop in 2024. The uncertainty of Keychange's future, partners and methods is mirrored in the uncertainty with which the project is presented online. Secondly, it is argued that the strategies for feminist gender equality work used by Keychange are diverse. This is a strength since Keychange can challenge different types of gender inequality affecting the music industries by addressing multiple problems and presenting multiple solutions.

Keychange

Keychange was launched in 2017 at Reeperbahn Music Festival in Germany; however, the collaboration between PRS Foundation, Musikcentrum Öst, Reeperbahn Festival, BIME, Tallinn Music Week and Iceland Airwaves had already started to develop in 2014. Keychange partners include popular music festivals in Europe and Canada, for example Tallinn Music Week, Iceland Airwaves, Way Out West and MUTEK. Keychange's focus on collaborating with festivals to develop gender equality within the music industries should be understood in the context of ongoing media debates about the lack of gender equality at music festivals in the 2010s. A few years ago, music festivals came to be at the centre of the media discussion about gender equality in popular music: (1) for the sexual harassment and rape of (mostly) female visitors at music festivals and (2) for the numerical gender balance in line-ups at festivals where male artists dominated. While neither sexual harassment nor male dominance on festival stages is new, sexual harassment at music festivals was articulated as an urgent problem and hit the international media circuit in 2016 and 2017 when sexual harassment and rape at Sweden's Bråvalla Festival were reported internationally, forcing the organizers to cancel the festival in

2018.¹ In 2017, the #MeToo movement exploded, and during the time leading up to the summer music festivals in Europe in 2018, sexual harassment at music festivals was in the news again. The media debates described a situation where mainly young girls were being sexually harassed and raped by mainly young men.² Notwithstanding, other genders including non-binary, trans people and cis men were possibly targeted too, in small numbers.³ During the same years, in the late 2010s, a discussion on how many women perform on the stages of popular music festival was ongoing in the media. The discussions often took as their starting point the numerical balance, with journalists counting the female artists on the posters and programmes of popular music festivals. One example of such an inquiry was a survey from 2016 published in *The Huffington Post*. The survey found that female artists accounted for 12 per cent of the acts at ten of the most popular US music festivals in 2016.⁴ The discussions on male dominance on stage at music festivals resurfaced in the media at the beginning of every festival season in the years to follow. In 2017, the BBC found that seven out of ten artists at UK popular music festivals were male solo artists or all male bands, and they included references to reports on similar findings by other journalists.⁵

When Keychange started at Reeperbahn Festival in September 2017, the media discussions about women on stage at music festivals and the treatment of female visitors were important contexts for the launch.⁶ The three original

---

¹ https://www.washingtonpost.com/news/worldviews/wp/2016/07/07/the-hideous-sexual-assault-problem-at-music-festivals-is-causing-major-tensions-in-europe/ and https://www.theguardian.com/world/2017/jul/03/swedens-bravalla-music-festival-cancelled-next-year-after-sex-attacks (both accessed 15 June 2021).
² https://www.bbc.com/news/entertainment-arts-44518892 and https://www.abc.net.au/triplej/programs/hack/how-common-is-sexual-violence-at-music-festivals/10425454 (both accessed 15 June 2021).
³ In this chapter, trans people is used to include all trans* identities, and non-binary is used as a complement to include those defined as such. The vocabulary changes and queer, gender-neutral or agender could also be included as gender identities outside of the binary men/women.
⁴ http://data.huffingtonpost.com/music-festivals (accessed 15 June 2021). The survey used four categories: female, male, mixed and other/unknown. The fourth category contained 60 artists (out of over 4,000) and is not reported on in the article.
⁵ https://www.bbc.com/culture/article/20190625-the-battle-for-gender-equal-festival-line-up (accessed 16 June 2021).
⁶ Keychange also uses media outlets to perform its work and spread the news about it: the websites analysed here, social media, traditional media, media technology used at the festivals where participants perform and the festivals' media channels. The role of mediation is thereby both a context and a tool in Keychange.

partners were figuring out a way to change music festivals, to make them more equal, with music festivals as the collaborators and their ideas interplayed with contemporary discussions. The funding that Keychange has received from Creative Europe, commercial sponsors and other partners also highlights that several types of actors see festivals as a central place to improve gender equality in the music industries. The project later grew to include several gender equality strategies, but started with the aim to put more female artists (50:50) on stage at music festivals and a career programme was developed in collaboration with festivals to achieve this goal by supporting the development of these artists.

The material in focus in this chapter is Keychange's online presentation of their aims, activities, methods and participants on four websites: Keychange's own website and the websites of PRS Foundation, Musikcentrum Öst and Reeperbahn Festival. These were selected because they are the three leading partners of the Keychange 2019–24 programme, and they all include information about the project online. The aim is to understand the kind of gender equality work that Keychange is undertaking and to discuss the strengths and weaknesses of their strategies from perspectives given in previous research studies on gender equality in the music industries. Further, the online material collected is contextualized with examples from the media debate about Keychange and gender balance as gender equality in the music industries. A feminist policy analysis (Bacchi 2009) is used to investigate the types of problems and solutions that Keychange is presenting for gender equality in music. Carol Bacchi (2009) has developed a type of discourse analysis labelled 'What's the problem' that is widely applied to policy in feminist scholarship. In her methodological outline, she argues that the presentation of what the problem is appears in the solutions offered in policy, written policy and policy in practice. She argues that presenting individualistic solutions (like job-seeking courses) to unemployment in certain groups (poor, Black or young, for example) signals that individuals are responsible for solving the problem of unemployment, and that their failure is their own fault. Not unlike the post-feminist critique discussed in Chapter 1, a feminist policy analysis focuses on the tension between structural and discursive feminist issues and individualistic solutions.

The chapter begins with a review and a discussion about previous studies on gender equality work in the music industries. Then, Keychange's feminist gender equality work is analysed in three sections: focusing first on the pledge and the participating sponsors and partners, second on the career programme and network for artists and innovators and finally on the Keychange manifesto that was presented to the European Parliament in 2018. The conclusion discusses the strengths of Keychange.

Organizing for gender equality in popular music

Gender equality goals have been included in cultural policy since the 1960s and are an important factor in all musical activity. How gender equality is imagined and pursued in cultural policy may look different depending on the historical, national and political context. In this chapter, research and discussion on practical gender equality work in the music industries are explained and used to critically discuss the potential of the Keychange project. According to Mary Celeste Kearney (2017: 126–7), working to achieve gender equality in the music industries has often had an educational framework where girls and women have been taught to become (popular music) musicians and artists. This has been done through settings where girls and women can learn to play, sing and compose without the presence of (cis) men. Institutes, schools, workshops and summer camps for girls and women (later also non-binary and trans people) are a long-standing tradition in music gender equality work and have been important efforts in creating safe spaces where girls and women may pursue an interest in playing rock music (later on other genres and producing). The idea behind such projects is that if girls/women are given the opportunity to develop their musical talent, they will become professional musicians in larger numbers. The lack of women in the music industries can (according to such thoughts) be rectified through educating the girls and women of the next generation, and gender inequality can be solved by the participation of women. This approach has been identified as having several weaknesses. It presents an individual solution – learning to play – to expressions of gender inequalities that are multifaceted. It fails to address structural and cultural problems in popular music and the music industries by assuming that just 'adding women' is going to help achieve change. The adding women approach to music history was discussed in the Introduction of the book as based on a liberal feminist tradition of thought.

Examples of educational framings for activities to develop gender equality in the popular music industries are workshops at Ladyfest, the Melbourne rock 'n' roll school for girls (1990–2002), and the most know example: Girls rock camps. Girls rock camps were started in 2001 in the United States by Misty McElroy. Today, the Girls Rock Camp Alliance brings together girls rock camps around the world, and rock is not the only genre practiced in the camps even though the name persists.[7] Paula Propst (2017) studied a girls rock camp in California and carried out interviews and ethnographic field work with participants. She concluded that the intergenerational dimensions of rock camps, where young participants meet older teachers, and the affective dimension of performing music together contribute to a felt empowerment for the participants of the camps. Andrea Dankić (2019) and Cecilia Björck (2011) have studied Popkollo, a Swedish rock camp for girls and a member of the Girls Rock Camp Alliance. Dankić (2019: 170) concludes that the camps she studied that train girls to write and perform hip hop not only empower participants, but also shape ideas about who can be a female rapper in terms of race, place, class and sometimes religion. Thus, the persons whom the camp aims to empower are also racialized and gendered in the learning process, as girls fulfilling, or not, the image of a possible rap artist, the experience co-existing with feelings of empowerment. Strategies employed by feminist activists at a girls rock camp have been studied by Danielle Giffort (2011) who argues that the feminist ideas behind the camps are often expressed in a vague or disguised manner for strategic reasons. In her study (Giffort 2011: 584), self-identified feminists worked within a feminist organization striving to bring gender equality to popular music but they did so without explicitly calling what they did feminist. The word 'feminism' became easier for artists, activists and fans to claim in popular music during the 2010s as discussed in the Introduction and Chapter 1. Giffort's results may be mirroring a passed relationship to feminism. Still, Keychange is not calling itself feminist either, but the analysis will show that a gender equality feminism is at the core of the methods for change that are used by Keychange.

---

[7] https://www.girlsrockcampalliance.org/ (accessed 14 May 2021).

Björck (2021: 38) has presented an overview of the ideas, strategies and conflicts in music's gender equality movements up to today. She argues that while twentieth-century gender equality movements focused on popular music, and rock in particular, the number of genres included in music's gender equality work has grown. According to Björck (2021: 33), the gender equality movements in music have also moved into the music industries, schools and higher music education, that are no longer dominated by non-profit grassroots organizations and projects. These findings, that gender equality is increasingly addressed in all genres and in established institutions of music while gender inequalities also persist, are supported by Sarah Raine and Catherine Strong (2019). Their work has collected research proving that gender equality was pursued by many institutions and in many countries during the 2010s. Keychange, initiated and led by interest organization PRS Foundation, Musikcentrum Öst a members' organization and Reeperbahn Festival a music industry commercial organization, also has several business sponsors (Soundcloud and Roskilde Festival, for example). While Keychange is not profit oriented, and neither are two out of the three organizations running it, many of its close collaborators are. This makes it hard to fully separate non-profit organizations from the commercially geared music industries when discussing Keychange. Björck (2021: 44) also argues that the strategies she has identified in music's gender equality movements are protectional, confrontational or administrative. The protectional strategies aim to promote safe spaces for women and girls (and sometimes also non-binary and trans people) to produce and play music. The confrontational strategies address inequalities in music with, for example, media activism, and the administrative strategies promote 'balance' in the music industries through gender mainstreaming work within the industries.[8] Her division is useful, and recent empirical examples show that the strategies often co-exist. For example, in the #MeToo

---

[8] Gender mainstreaming was discussed and defined in the introduction as an internationally adopted strategy for gender equality that involves integrating a gender perspective into the preparation, design, implementation, monitoring and evaluation of policies, regulatory measures and spending programmes. Creative Europe, funding Keychange, is using the European Union (EU) tool kit for gender mainstreaming.

petition discussed in Chapter 2, a protectional space for discussion was first created on Facebook. Then the confrontational petition was published in the media which, in its turn, could lead to the revision of policy and practice in the Swedish music industry (through administrative solutions). Keychange also employs multiple strategies in gender equality work where the career programme is both protectional and administrative, and the pledge and the manifesto are confrontational, encouraging administrative solutions.

After many decades of gender equality movements, the music industries are still male dominated (Smith et al. 2021), and feminist strategies have expanded efforts aimed at affecting the music industries in more ways than just educational initiatives. For example, changing the policies that govern the music industries and building collectives of artists for community-based change. Keychange is an example of such work that aims to change the industries from within, music festivals first, and to showcase talent (not teach girls to play the guitar). As discussed in the Introduction, gender mainstreaming in the creative industries has been pursued in different parts of Europe. The European Union's gender mainstreaming strategies have influenced policy in several European countries. Sam de Boise (2019) discusses how gender equality in music is pursued in Sweden and the UK, arguing that an ideal of 'balance' between, primarily, the genders of performers is often put forward as the goal of gender mainstreaming. The genders are further constructed as binary, men and women, and gender mainstreaming is, according to de Boise (2019), looking less to the business side of the music industries for example, or the musical content performed on stage. This critique of gender mainstreaming finds similar weaknesses in the approach as those discussed in the case of the equalizer in Chapter 3.

In another study, Sarah Raine (2020) has investigated the outcomes of gender equality work at the Cheltenham Jazz Festival. After taking the Keychange pledge, the festival committed to reach a 50:50 gender balance on their festival's stages. She concludes that the 'one woman on stage' goal, which categorizes an act as 'female' if there is one woman on stage, is a flawed instrument for achieving gender equality. According to Keychange's 'one woman on stage' way of measuring a 50:50 gender balance, the gender equality aim could be met if ten bands with ten members performed and five of them had one female singer, making the number of women 5 per cent, 5 women out of 100 performers, but counting it as 50 per cent. The way the Cheltenham Jazz Festival reached its goal for gender balance does not account for the actual numerical gender representation on stage (or off stage), and maybe more importantly it obscures the roles that women take on stage (often as vocalists in male-dominated jazz bands), and it does not account for the experiences of working at the festival as a female jazz musician. Raine (2020) mapped the gender representation on the festival's stage and performed qualitative interviews with ten female musicians performing at the Cheltenham Jazz Festival in 2019. She (2020: 17) concluded that sexual harassment, educational barriers and knowledge gaps were perceived as very important areas to address if one wants to achieve gender equality in UK jazz. The musicians participating in the interviews were hesitant about the effects of the Keychange pledge on gender equality at the festival. And the critique raised by Raine of the effectiveness of the 'one woman on stage' policy in combatting the experienced problems for female musicians needs to be kept in mind.

As discussed in Chapter 3, an integrating gender mainstreaming strategy (Squires 2005), aiming only to increase the numbers of participating women, is limited in what it can achieve. While it is easy to understand and it is easy to measure its success, integrating gender mainstreaming fails to address the structure and culture of the organization that needs to change, such as sexism, and other qualitative experiences of mistreatment in the music industries. It also fails to recognize the terms of inclusion and the positions the women included can occupy. On the other hand, being invited to perform and participate in festivals and live venues is crucial to build a career. Putting more female, non-binary and trans artists on festival stages would benefit their careers, even if participating is not enough. In the following analysis, the history of Keychange, the programme, the pledge and the manifesto will be discussed as they are presented online.

How it started

Keychange is a collaboration between interest and members' organizations: PRS Foundation (UK) and Musikcentrum Öst (Sweden), together with music industry conferences and popular music festivals: first and foremost, the third lead organization Reeperbahn Festival (Germany). It all started with Vanessa Reed, the then CEO of PRS Foundation, and another initiative of PRS Foundation that was started before Keychange: 'Women make music', a programme supporting women, trans and non-binary composers and songwriters. 'Women make music' started in 2010 for composers and songwriters in the UK and Vanessa Reed wanted to broaden PRS Foundation's ambition for gender equality in the music industries to include support for artists, not only composers.[9] At the Womex Festival in Spain in 2014, Vanessa Reed and Ragnar Berthling from Musikcentrum Öst discussed expanding a similar international programme for artists.[10] Vanessa Reed was responsible for getting Alexander Schulz from Reeperbahn Festival and representatives from Estonia, Iceland and Spain onboard, making Keychange a six-nation partnership. In 2015, they applied for funding from Creative Europe, but they were rejected. The second application formulated clearer activities called 'creative labs' for the artists participating in the career programme and in early 2017, Keychange received the first grant. Keychange was launched in September 2017 at Reeperbahn Festival. The Creative Europe Programme of the European Union is the main funder of Keychange (in two funding periods) that now consists of three parts: a career development programme to promote individual music talents; a pledge to change the music industries to achieve a 50:50 gender balance for music industry actors to sign; and a manifesto aimed at changing policy affecting gender equality in the music industries.

In the 2019–24 programme, Keychange is professionalized with a board, yearly meetings, employed staff and well-defined roles in the management team. As you will see below, it employs different strategies and activities, and it exists in the larger context of the Creative Europe Programme of the European Union that has funded gender mainstreaming initiatives in music around Europe.

The main work of Keychange is carried out within the career development programme that conducts workshops and meetings for all participating

---

[9] In 2010, it supported 'women composers and songwriters'.
[10] Source material for the background of Keychange is an interview with Ragnar Berthling from Musikcentrum Öst.

female, trans and non-binary artists (the second programme includes innovators – persons innovating in the music industry in other ways than as artists). In addition to the career development programme, Keychange aims to build a network where participants can continue to utilize each other after they have finished the programme and are building a career in the music industries. The pledge was developed in 2017, making it possible for organizations that were not partners or sponsors to support Keychange's aim: gender equality formulated as a 50:50 balance in the music industries. The manifesto was an outcome of the first career programme that ended in 2018. It built on the discussions held in workshops during the first programme, voicing the ideas of the artists participating in Keychange. In 2019, Keychange applied for and received their second Creative Europe grant, now with eleven full partners, twelve countries and thirteen festivals in collaboration. The second Keychange programme was intended as a four-year programme but has, at the time of writing, been delayed due to the Covid-19 pandemic that started in 2020. It has been changed to run from 2019 to 2024.[11] During 2020, webinars were held, and social media has been used to keep the Keychange programme alive.

A programme for career development

According to all the websites, the main output of Keychange is 'the programme', which is described as developing talents, artists and innovators from underrepresented genders to take their place in the music industries. Artists and innovators can apply to take part in the programme where they are supported with travel grants, organized network meetings, workshops and, on completion of the programme, a booking to perform at one of the partner festivals. This booking is the programme's way of supporting the artists with an opportunity to perform on a major stage and show off their music and talent. The partner festivals are crucial in selecting the participants of the programme.

---

[11] At the time of writing in September 2021.

The first Keychange programme was launched in 2017, but all the activities were conducted in 2018. The second round of the Keychange programme was launched in 2019 and was supposed to take place throughout 2020 but has been delayed by the pandemic that has prevented travel, workshops and festivals from taking place except online.[12] The programme also aims to support and develop the participants' music-related careers by building a network of Keychange artists and innovators who will support each other in their future, prolonging its effects after the programme has ended. Applicants must be of an 'under-represented gender' and 'undiscovered' – thus no already established artists or innovators.

This section of the chapter discusses how the websites gender and value the participants of the programme, and what this way of constructing them says about Keychange's gender equality work. The programme's content – what happens during workshops and meetings – is not explained on the websites. The programme participants are presented as crucial for Keychange – they therefore *become* the programme as representative subjects on how it is presented online.

While rock camps for girls are often aimed at amateurs looking to develop their skills in playing and writing music, the career programme that Keychange offers is aimed at talents in music who are already active and excellent at what they do but need to thrive or break through. Keychange's website describes the participants as already talented, and a 'unique talent' used on the first page of Keychange.eu signifies the artists joining Keychange. The visitor to the Keychange website is encouraged to nominate 'undiscovered talent' to the career programme. Under 'our roster' where the artists and innovators are presented individually with photographs and biographical texts, they are described as having 'outstanding talent'. The word 'talent' is used many times, and it implies that someone has a lot of potential to become great, for example in music, but is not yet famous, has not yet reached the destination of that

---

[12] Participating as a researcher in the programme would have contributed to analysing Keychange's given problems and solutions for gender equality work in the music industries. The pandemic made this impossible, and even though I followed online activities on social media, this chapter focuses on the websites.

talent, is not yet great. Being talented is, rhetorically, being on one's way to being good at something.

The idea of talent has previously been used to dismiss critiques of gender inequality in popular music, arguing that talent, not gender, should be in focus. Tami Gadir (2017) takes as her starting point the Norwegian popular music festival Musikkfest booking four females out of forty-seven DJs in 2016, to discuss ideas about talent and freedom in popular music culture. She (2017: 65) argues that the idea of talent as surpassing gender is used to dispute critiques of gender inequality in popular music among DJs in Norway. Arguments from DJ culture participants and bookers contend that they did not book DJs based on gender, they booked talent without seeing gender. This can be understood as implicitly saying that female DJs are not that good if booking practices see talent and book men. The idea of talent as grounds for being booked and ideas about everyone's freedom to pursue their talent (ibid.) cover up structural inequalities in a DJ scene that really works like a boy's club, a network for men, according to the female DJs whom Gadir interviewed. When Keychange is developing 'talent', this emphasis can be seen as a response to such a critique of gender equality. By highlighting talent, Keychange incorporates the critique and deflates it. Under-represented genders are invited *because* they are talented. Talent is represented as something individual and possible for an artist to develop, but everyone's freedom to develop their talent in the same manner is disputed. Keychange clearly presents that there are challenges to developing one's talent for under-represented genders. Not being booked is presented as not their own fault but a consequence of the cis male-dominated music industries. In the FAQ section of the Keychange website under the questions concerning 'gender minorities', the artists and innovators are described as people who have 'encountered barriers'. While the exact nature of these barriers is not described, the wording indicates that Keychange recognizes not only individual but also structural problems. Keychange presents solutions for developing individual talent that not only focus on the individual. When artists and innovators are put on stage, they are also working with others and in networks against structural hinderance that is recognized (Figure 4.1).

There are several ways of understanding how the artists and innovators are put forward as valuable for popular music in Keychange's work, and

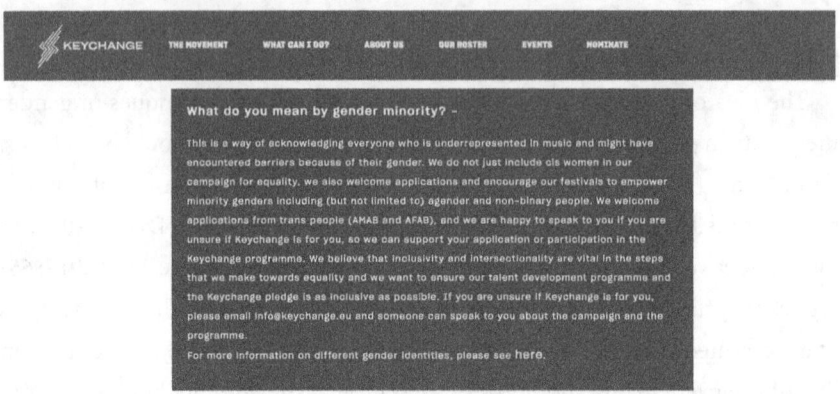

Figure 4.1 The term 'gender minority' as explained on the Keychange.eu website in 2021 (screenshot by the author).

'talent' is not the only term used. On Musikcentrum Öst's website, 'potential and originality' are words describing the participants; PRS Foundation uses 'emergent artists'; and on the Reeperbahn Festival website 'talented' is used again. There is active meaning making around who the participants of the Keychange programme are and what characteristics are the driving force of the gender equality project. They are described as talented, with potential, original or emergent as part of constructing the persons who will solve the problem: they are great enough to be the change that Keychange wants to achieve and help the music industries to reach a 50:50 gender balance. Christina Scharff (2015) has argued that for professional musicians today the language and practice of self-promoting are important. Promoting yourself as an excellent musician is difficult for the female musicians she interviewed because they are women. Scharff (2015: 109) argues that this is because it may be perceived as too pushy for a female musician to promote herself, and it can also be seen as unartistic or even associated with selling one's body. When Keychange symbolically constructs the participants of their programme as talented and with potential, the participants are imagined as artists and innovators who are on their way to great future careers in music. They may *already* be understood as excellent artists by the Keychange programme, but have not managed to sell themselves as 'excellent' and get the attention and 'showcase' that they deserve. The career programme offers to help them shape a career and reach the success that they deserve in collective collaboration with other artists. The potential, talent, originality and excellent qualities described on the websites do not conflict with femininity because the participants are not themselves pushing their work as 'excellent', 'the best', 'perfect' or any similar confident language. Keychange is presented as performing this pushing for them and the term 'to showcase' the talented participants joining the programme is used. Keychange will help them enter the marketplace by showcasing them at festivals without the participants having to brag. This means that Keychange is the agent that helps the artists reach the next level – and they are constructed as in need of help.

The solution that Keychange offers is not individualistic, there is a group of people at Keychange and there is a collective of artists presented as such on the website. The collective of artists is clearly presented; nevertheless, it is important to note that exactly what Keychange is, what funding it has, what employees work there, who is on the board and so on are hard to learn from the online information. The helping hand is thus undefined. The artists and innovators are imagined as receiving access to networks through the Keychange programme, networks they take with them after the programme that will help them build a career in the long term. The programme aims to build long-term change in the participants' careers.

Gendering the participants of the programme

The gender of the participants of Keychange is described as crucial since the aim is to change the dominance of cis males in the music industries. How the artists and innovators are gendered differs in the material collected from the websites. The four ways to describe the gender of (wanted) participants are women, under-represented genders, gender minorities and trans*, non-binary, agender and female. A question raised on the Keychange FAQ page of the Reeperbahn Festival website is 'What about transgender and non-binary performers and professionals?' The answer is that Keychange includes trans* and non-binary in the 50 per cent of women on stage goal. Thus, all genders that are not cis male are included on one side of the 50:50 balance according to this answer. Still the headline of the page is 'Keychange empowering women in music'.

Under 'the movement' on the Keychange website, the artists and innovators supported by the programme are simply described as 'under-represented artists' with no mention of their gender; however, in the same sentence, Keychange is encouraging organizations to take a pledge for gender equality (Figure 4.2). This formulation can be interpreted as 'under-represented' artists being women, or women and other under-represented genders, depending on the reader's knowledge and understanding of the possible genders. Also, next to this text there is an image of (assumed) participants and most of them look like young women even though their self-defined gender identity is not certain from my visual examination. While the intention of using 'under-represented artists' instead of gendering the artists clearly may be to include all gender identities outside the cis male norm, the presentation of the movement on the Keychange website does not clearly include trans and non-binary people or focus on gender. It could be interpreted as under-represented for other reasons, like class, race, sexuality or ethnicity.

On PRS Foundation's website under 'partnerships' and 'keychange' a photograph of a person with unclear gender (could be interpreted as a woman, trans, non-binary person or a feminine cis man) illustrates the text

Figure 4.2 Keychange is presented as a movement with words and a photo on the Keychange.eu website in 2021 (screenshot by the author).

about Keychange. The person is not named. In the text beside the photograph, Keychange is described as striving to 'include women and under-represented genders' (Figure 4.3). Here, in PRS Foundation's presentation of Keychange there are multiple genders that can be under-represented, not just women. It is not spelled out what those genders are, but it is made clear that this gender equality effort does not exclude trans and non-binary people. Also, since women and under-represented genders are separate, it is not clear that women are under-represented in the music industries. This phrasing is sending a different message than the previously discussed gendered presentation of artists on the Keychange website. If one turns to the FAQ section on the Keychange website, which is shown in Figure 4.1, looking for answers about what a 'gender minority' is, it is explained as agender, non-binary and trans people. There is also a link to stonewall.org.uk for an extensive list of terms regarding sexuality and gender identity.[13] The list defines sexualities, gender identities and biologically defined categories like intersex people. The list has the effect of furthering the confusion between ideas about sexuality and gender identity. The sexualities of artists and innovators are not addressed anywhere else on the Keychange website, rather 'inclusivity and intersectionality' are used in the same section as the question 'what do you mean by gender minority?'.

As discussed in the introduction, intersectional feminist theory is concerned with the co-construction of gender with other social and cultural categories like class, race and sexuality. Most often, key theoretical discussions have engaged with the importance of intersections of gender, race and class in the United States, reflecting the Black feminist theoretical roots of the concept (Crenshaw 1991). 'Gender minorities' is not a category based on intersectional understandings of gender, since the interplay between gender and other categories is not highlighted: gender is in focus. Class, race/ethnicity and sexuality are not mentioned explicitly on the Keychange website, but intersectionality as a concept is mentioned and it may be understood as a desire to address these sociocultural categories

---

[13] https://www.stonewall.org.uk/help-advice/faqs-and-glossary/glossary-terms (accessed 16 June 2021).

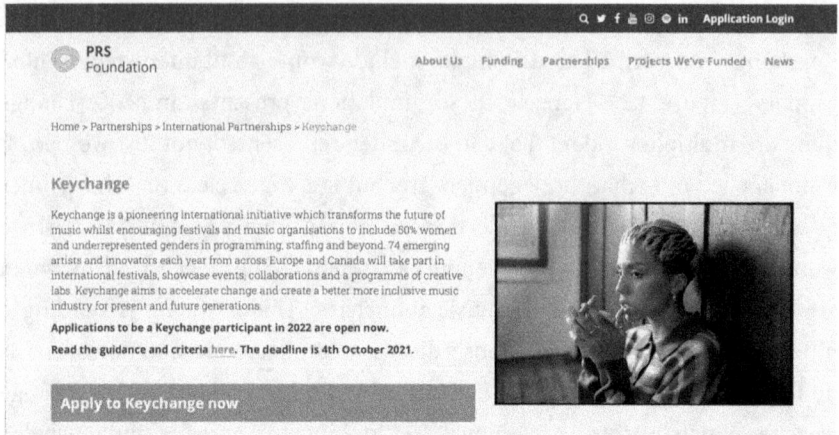

Figure 4.3 What Keychange is as explained on the PRS Foundation's website, prsfoundation.com, in 2021 (screenshot by the author).

together. The Reeperbahn Festival defines the participants, besides female artists, as 'transgender and non-binary', which is the clearest formulation of what genders other than women are present among the artists included in the Keychange programme.

The statistics and research presented by Keychange on the website as background for the need to change the music industries often use the terms 'men' and 'women' as the sole gender categories. Keychange also presents 'Friday figures' every week on their website and on social media (Facebook, Twitter and Instagram) as a way of framing statistics about gender in music. The Friday figures are diverse and put forward both positive results, when women, trans and non-binary artists are joining the music industries, and negative results from recent surveys that support the claim that these are under-represented genders in the music industries. Keychange has not created the statistical results that are presented in the Friday figures, they draw on several sources, and Keychange does not control how gender is defined in them. Nevertheless, the gender of the subjects that Keychange speaks to and about are defined in multiple ways between the websites, creating some confusion. The confusion about what gender is could also be transformative in how it refuses to pin gender down to a number of given categories.

The descriptions of the programme participants, their talent and gender are part of how the solution to gender inequality is constructed by Keychange, because the persons taking part in the programme, as individuals and as a collective, are presented as being the solution to the under-representation of female, non-binary and trans artists in the music industries. During their careers, they will change the music industries and further gender equality and it is therefore crucial who they are since gender equality is measured by the people included. It is not fully clear what genders the Keychange programme supports when Musikcentrum Öst writes about 'female talent', Keychange about 'under-represented artists', the Reeperbahn Festival about 'women and gender minorities' and PRS Foundation about 'women and under-represented genders' (Figure 4.4). The gender of the participants is not always clear in the material, but they are talented and progressing all the time, needing networks, tools and exposure on stage to reach their career goals.

While all genders except cis male are seemingly welcome in the Keychange programme, if one reads these definitions and no discussions about race and ethnicity are made explicit on the websites, underlying values possibly expressed in the terms 'originality' and 'intersectionality' are manifesting themselves in

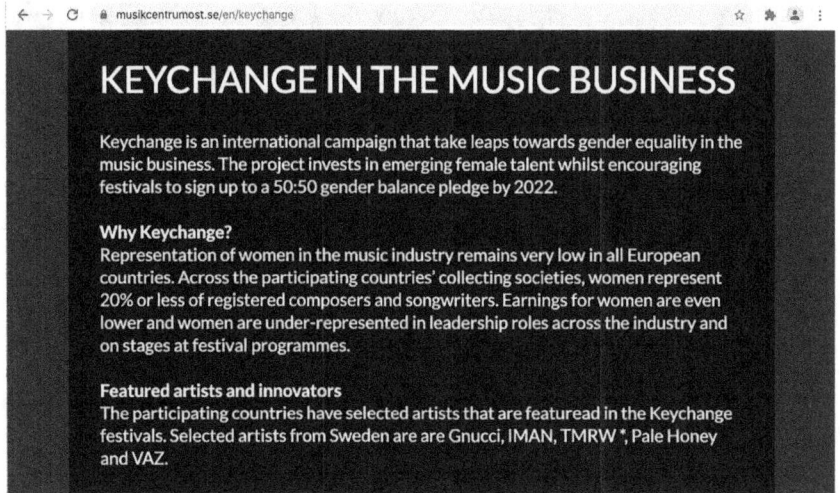

Figure 4.4 What Keychange is as explained on the Musikcentrum Öst's website, musikcentrumost.se, in 2021 (screenshot by the author).

the roster of artists. Women dominate in the roster of Keychange artists and innovators, but there are non-binary artists (Kimmortal for example) and gender-mixed groups (Isák for example) stressing that under-represented genders are not interpreted by Keychange as only 'women', perhaps even cis men are welcome if the group they are part of contains several genders. The roster has a high representation of Black and brown artists, judging from the photos, and of different genres, judging from how the music is described, but mainstream pop is not heavily represented, indicating that originality and talent are found outside of chart pop music. Mainstream pop is generally the genre with the highest representation of female artists and it is also symbolically associated with femininity – regarding trans and binary artists there is not enough research to substantiate what genres they are perceived to be participating in.

A pledge for gender equality

The Keychange pledge was put together when Keychange was launched in Germany in 2017. It received a lot of interest from representatives of the music industries, record labels in particular, and later on other actors that could not be partner festivals. The pledge also received a lot of media attention. It was cited as '50:50 by 2022', where 50:50 is a measurement of the desirable gender balance (first female/male and later explained as cis male/women and minority genders) in the music industries and 2022 was the year when this should be achieved.[14] Since this book is published in 2022, the goal '50:50 by 2022' now seems unrealistic, which may have been the case already in 2017 when the term was coined. And the term is very catchy.

On Reeperbahn Festival's website under Keychange FAQs the pledge is explained as '50:50 in line-ups of popular music festivals will be measured

---

[14] The '50:50 by 2022' formulation of the pledge has been removed from the Keychange website. However, was circulating in 2019 as seen in an article in *the Guardian* (https://www.theguardian.com/world/2019/jun/25/music-industry-urged-to-join-campaign-for-gender-parity (accessed 9 June 2021).

according to the number of acts featuring at least one self-identifying woman, transgender or non-binary individual'. This explanation of the pledge is specific in stating what should be achieved by festivals to meet their pledge. With this definition, a jazz band with one female/trans/non-binary singer becomes a 'female' act, as observed by Raine (2020). In 2021, the pledge was presented on the Keychange website as more complex than earlier media discussions had let on. Under 'what can I do as a music organization?', the pledge has a list of eight suggested actions that differ between orchestras, concert halls, conservatoires, agents, publishers and labels, charities and trade bodies, broadcasters, publications employing editorial staff, organizations with youth groups and educational programmes. While the 50:50 target is still mentioned in one of the suggested pledges, it is not emphasized; instead the website states: 'we strongly believe that the target needs to be defined and owned by the festivals and organizations themselves'.

The list of suggested pledges does, however, focus on participants and not content. It is the artists on stage, the composers, the backstage staff, the board members and so on, and not the content of the music, performances, or images that an organization can pledge to change to improve the gender equality of the music industries. As discussed in Chapter 3, there is no guarantee that female artists will not promote sexism, homophobia or racism in their work and artist personas. De Bois (2019) has argued that gender mainstreaming by numbers and efforts to increase the number of women and sometimes trans and non-binary people in music tend to focus on performers, the people who we see on stage. This critique seems to have been taken on board by Keychange in the project's list with suggestions for pledges that organizations can make. The suggested actions diversify not only the artists but also the people, organizations and institutions involved in making music happen. Genres are also diversified in the pledge as it appears on the website in 2021. While Keychange in the early days focused on popular music, orchestras, conservatoires and organizations for classical music are now mentioned as organizations that might want to take the Keychange pledge. The artists participating in the Keychange programme are limited in music genre by the profiles of the festivals showcasing them that are important in the process of selecting artists, but innovators are not limited by genre in the Keychange programme. The focus on popular music among many of the partner festivals may give the idea of Keychange as limited to popular music.

The reason given on the Keychange website for taking the pledge is the low percentage of 'women and gender minorities in the music industry' in European countries. As has been discussed above, the numbers given to substantiate these claims are mostly counting women and men. Contextualizing Keychange in Europe fits well with the funding that Keychange has received from Creative Europe, the main funder of Keychange's programme. Sponsors also fund Keychange, but the size and the nature of their contributions are unclear according to what one learns from the website. Canada is also a member country through the MUTEK Festival and there have been discussions about US partners joining. The main argument in the motif given for taking the pledge is to challenge the uneven gender balance. The idea of 'a gender-balanced music industry' as a good aim colours the introduction to the pledge. Why balance would be good is not presented nor discussed. Additionally, the pledge omits other possible grounds of imbalance in the music industries such as race, sexuality, functionality and class. The pledge's widening of the roles in music work – from artists to much more – should be understood in the context of a discussion in research on gender and music using the analysis of the music industries as systems (Leonard 2007). Marion Leonard (2007) has argued that music industry professionals like journalists, sound engineers and promoters take part in shaping gender in the music industries. In her work, the gender of professionals in the music industries should be less in focus than the 'how': how they construct ideas about masculinity and femininity in music. Leonard (2007: 4) calls this a gendered culture of indie rock, an analysis transferable to other genres. Using works like Leonard's and seeing the music industries as building gendered cultures, researchers have furthered discussions about some areas that are highly masculinized: for example, studio work and all types of music production (Wolf 2020, Reddington 2021). Learning from this feminist research on the music industries teaches us that gender is more than the gender identity of artists. Gendered culture exists in all parts of the music industries. Some activities are gendered as more masculine than others and those parts of music work would benefit from feminist analysis. In the pledge, the definition of several organizations, roles and actions supports this understanding of gender in the music industries.

A manifesto to change policy

The first round of the Keychange programme resulted in a manifesto that was presented to the European Parliament in late 2018 (Keychange PRS Foundation 2018). The manifesto was written by the three main partners and was based on discussions with all participants of the first programme. These discussions took place after every festival that Keychange was involved with in the 2018 round of the Keychange programme. In the manifesto, Keychange is introduced and gender inequality in the music industries is highlighted as the motif of the project using statistics from different sources. After this introduction, four core areas in need of improvement to reach gender equality in the music industries are presented: working conditions and lack of senior role models, investment, research and education. The manifesto not only addresses the music industries with suggestions for change, but it also addresses national governments, the European Parliament and the European Commission as agents of change affecting the European music industries. Some of the actions suggested in the manifesto are ambitious. For example, the manifesto suggests implementing paid and shared parental leave and policies against sexist marketing in all nation states of the EU, plus the UK. Other examples of actions that the music industries are 'called on' to undertake are anonymizing the recruitment of staff, addressing the gender pay gap and adopting policies against sexual harassment.[15] The manifesto includes twenty-six actions that Keychange is calling on different actors to take. They differ internally; where some are vague: 'address the gender pay gap' (for the music industries), others are specific: 'commission a research study on the gender

---

[15] Feminist demands to stop sexual harassment in the music industries are discussed in Chapter 2. The occurrence of sexual misconduct in music work is impossible to deny, as there are regular revelations of such misconduct. The latest one is from the talent show *The Voice*. https://www.bbc.com/news/entertainment-arts-60022641 (accessed 26 January 2022).

balance and diversity of Europe's music industries and the economic benefits of increasing diversity'.

Unlike in the Keychange programme, where by entering the music industries the participants themselves are presented as solutions to gender inequality in the music industries, the manifesto's reform focuses on factors creating 'under-representation'. The manifesto locates problems and solutions on several different levels with the overall aim to make the music industries, national governments and the EU fight under-representation in music. Not only are general laws and policies around equal pay and parental leave pointed out as important for gender equality but also softer and more achievable suggestions like mentoring programmes (directed at the music industries) and organizing a meeting about gender balance (directed at the European Parliament) are brought forward. Some of the structural actions suggested to be taken by governments, parental leave for example, may be at odds with the political will in many EU countries. Addressing the gender pay gap and changing the recruitment processes in the music industries could potentially be costly reforms and at odds with the driving force of the business world: capitalism. In the manifesto, economic factors are understandably not in focus, but the capitalist driving force of the music industries is obscured when the different actors are put next to each other without definitions and differentiation. The manifesto delivers all of Squires (2005) three types of gender mainstreaming work: integrating, agenda setting and transformative, as discussed in Chapter 3. Integrating gender mainstreaming work called for in the manifesto includes that equal numbers of male and female experts should assess applications for EU funding programmes in the fields of culture and education. Another action suggested by the manifesto that can be considered transformative is its proposal that the music industries changes its recruitment processes and the culture of its organizations.

The language used in the manifesto is demanding rather than suggesting: 'we call on the music industry to' is the semantic way these actions are put forward by the manifesto and this rhetorical approach gives the manifesto a strict tone. In the manifesto, the concepts women, female and male are used and no other genders are mentioned. This binary construct does not reflect the multiple gender concepts presented by Keychange on its website that were discussed earlier in the chapter. The gender terminology of the manifesto creates some confusion about who the subject of Keychange is when compared to the genders presented online. In the manifesto, the focus on talent, originality and potential is also largely missing. The manifesto is from 2018 and the websites were analysed in 2021. One reason for the different constructions of the subjects that are unrepresented (problem) and will change the music industries by entering them (solution) may be time. Keychange developed the terminology in the second programme that started in 2019. There is no mention on any of the websites about how the manifesto was received by the EU, or if it has had any impact on the European Parliament. The manifesto still shows that Keychange's ideas about how gender equality can be achieved are more diverse than those seen in the programme and the pledge. The manifesto highlights that the Keychange project is not enough in itself and the project's managers are also lobbying for multiple changes in the industries, nations and on a European level. Keychange is planning to write a second manifesto that will be presented in 2024 on completion of the second programme.

What is Keychange's solution to gender inequality in music?

On the Keychange website under 'about us/who we are', Keychange's core actions are presented as the programme, the pledge and the manifesto, similar to the way they are presented in Figure 4.5. These are the three types of actions that Keychange takes for gender equality, but what kind of organization is it that is acting? Who is the agent of change, besides the participants in the programme? On Musikcentrum Öst's website, Keychange is called an 'international campaign'; on Keychange's own website it is presented not only as a 'movement' but also a 'programme' in the FAQ section; on Reeperbahn Festival's website, Keychange is a 'global network and movement'; and on PRS Foundation's website, Keychange is an 'international initiative'. Adopting the term 'movement' connotes social movements and grassroot organizations working for social change, which describes Keychange's aim but at the same

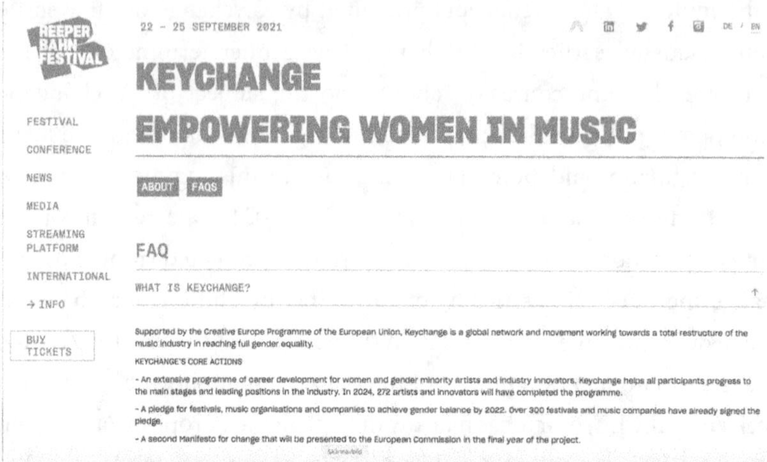

Figure 4.5 What Keychange is as explained on the Reeperbahn Festival website, reeperbahnfestival.com, in 2021 (screenshot by the author).

time it obscures Keychange's entanglement with the commercial music industries and with the political power of EU governing bodies.

In this chapter, I have opted to call Keychange a 'project' run by three main partner organizations: PRS Foundation, Musikcentrum Öst and Reeperbahn Festival. The partner organizations seem to be putting in equal amounts of work and use Reeperbahn Festival as a stage and a meeting place. Keychange does not have its own permanent organizational structure or employees. The people who work with Keychange are employed by one of the three partner organizations. Creative Europe, the main funding body, provides project funding for a few years at a time. The budget and the economic structure of Keychange are hidden from view in the material analysed here. But when Creative Europe is pointed out as the main funding body, it seems likely that Keychange is at risk of disappearing if the funding from Creative Europe stops since Keychange does not have an independent organizational or financial structure. It is also possible that Keychange will develop into something more permanent in the future and secure other types of funding, from the partners themselves or from sponsors. This uncertainty about Keychange's structure, longevity, funding and organizational form is the social context of the language uncertainty about what Keychange is that is presented on the websites.

Trying to understand how the project is organized, who is included, what the aim is and how the aim is going to be achieved is difficult for the researcher. Keychange is multiple things and the strategies and methods, as well as the language describing them are diverse. This confusion can be a strength since it makes Keychange difficult to contest and different types of gender inequality problems could potentially require different methods of change. If Keychange was clearly formulating one solution to the problem of the under-representation of female, trans and non-binary artists, then the weaknesses would be more obvious.

When presenting its problems and solutions, Keychange is not calling itself 'feminist', yet feminist ideology is clearly behind the idea that the under-representation of women, trans and non-binary people is a problem. In Giffort's (2011) study in which participants in a girls rock camp did not call their work feminist, which was understood by Giffort as strategic, feminism was perceived as something that might scare people away. Keychange's presentation of the problem (the under-representation of women, non-binary, trans artists) is based on a feminist analysis. Not using the word 'feminist' is beneficial when influencing people in positions of power who may react negatively to feminism but would find it hard to contest that 'under-representation' is a problem in general. Engaging with feminism and its theoretically different strands might help develop Keychange's analysis of why there is so much under-representation in the music industries. It is also possible that such work with feminist theory is done (or planned to be done) in the workshops with participants of the programme. Also, structural difficulties like pay inequality and parental leave are identified, and from Keychange's point of view the solution to these is lobbying with a manifesto aiming to affect policy in those areas (and others). The lobbying is directed towards the European Parliament, a governing body that has the authority to change policy.

Analysing the individualistic approach of Keychange's core action, the career programme that aims to showcase participants on festival stages, the online presentations are struggling to name who should be included; under-represented genders, gender minorities or women are mentioned in the material discussed above. 'Inclusion and diversity' are terms used that indicate that sociocultural categories other than gender may be important too. An inclusion of difference in nationality, race and genre is visible in the Keychange roster where participants' photos and biographies are found – this creates an image of Keychange taking race, ethnicity and nationality into account in the selection process. The Keychange roster displays mostly young women, gendered female by pronouns, who perform music or organize music-related activities and it presents them as very talented, even exceptional. The subjects that should be included on the stages are therefore constructed as *mostly* women. The emphasis on talent implies that these subjects can succeed, given the right tools and a stage at a festival. The flaw in this argument is the individualization of change, and the lack of a feminist critical examination of what 'talent' is. Talent and musical quality are not explored, for example, as possible sites or barriers through sexism or racism or genre rules. But Keychange does not stop with the programme for individuals. The programme is also presented as creating a network for the participants where the collective and not the individual is the force that can change the music industries. This solution is based on collective political power building a community for female, non-binary and trans artists in the music industries.

In the pledge and the manifesto, the solutions to gender equality are placed outside of Keychange's own programme, requiring institutions, like a record company, a national government or the EU Parliament, to act. The manifesto calls on several institutions to participate in changing inequality in music work and the updated pledge on the Keychange website also addresses both music businesses and state-run institutions, like concert halls and educational institutions, in higher music education. The music industries are considered multiple in contemporary scholarly discussion, consisting of, for example, the recording industry, performance-oriented institutions like venues and festivals, music technology companies, the media used for listening, television shows focusing on music and talent, the infrastructure used by artists such as booking agents and the media (including social media) reporting on music. In the formulation of the pledge on the Keychange website in 2021, the multiplicity of the music industries is represented. Keychange asks organizations to outline their own goals when signing the pledge, indicating that Keychange has identified a weakness in telling all organizations to do the same thing: a 50:50 balance of genders on stage. This is a response to Raine's (2020) findings where the female artists in UK jazz whom she spoke to considered sexual harassment, educational barriers and knowledge gaps important problems to address to promote gender equality in music. They did not consider the festival's gender-balanced stages a success even though they look right on paper. The amended pledge suggested by Keychange in 2021 requires actions shaped by the problems of the organizations joining, and the organizations are required to do more than just sign and balance participation. They need to identify their own gender equality issues, which is an important step.

Conclusion

The Keychange project has one major strength in how it is defining the problems of and the solutions to gender inequality in the music industries: it offers multiple solutions backed up with multiple activities and other actions. Using Bacchi's (2009) terminology, the problems that Keychange policy points to are multiple, shown in the multiple solutions that Keychange presents. For example, the solution to create networks for female (non-binary and trans) artists is identified by Keychange and has also been identified in research (Leonard 2007). The impact of the networking practices examined by Leonard (2007) studying the Riot Grrrl scene was significant for participating female musicians. Keychange aims to build a network, or even a community, that will outlive the programme and further gender equality in the long term as a collective strategy. The problem the network responds to is a sexist culture in the music industries where female, non-binary and trans artists are excluded from existing networks. To function, it uses online sites and social media, but physical meetings and friendships between participants, as well as a feeling of belonging to the Keychange movement, are at the core of how Keychange aims to build a network.

Further, the way the music industries structures work, workplace cultures, the gender pay gap and recruitment practices, is challenged in the Keychange manifesto, and the demand for diversity and inclusion in the policy asks for more than a 50:50 gender balance. The problems and the solutions of Keychange are quantitative and qualitative, making the gender equality work the project performs more effective since it addresses gender inequality as diverse – with diverse roads to equality. As discussed above, the part of the programme that focuses on developing individual artists and innovators' talents and showcasing them to the music industries and audiences, is an individualistic solution that presents gender equality as an individualistic problem. It is important to note here that individualistic career developments are put in context by the multiple solutions that Keychange presents. The gender equality work that Keychange performs should be understood as a whole, where the solutions complement each other.

Finally, I want to turn to the capitalist logic of the music industries that may prevent many of the suggestions in the manifesto. As hinted at earlier in the chapter, Keychange collaborates with businesses as well as governing organizations. Abolishing all sexist marketing could be understood as a very costly reform as much of the music industries' marketing builds on stereotypes of gender and race. Neoliberal capitalist ideology and its relation to contemporary-mediated popular music has been an underlying topic in all the empirical chapters in this book. Capitalism is interlinked with the mainstream of popular music and with much gender equality work: in the European Union gender equality reforms are often put forward with the argument that gender equality will bring about economic growth and a stronger workforce by including women. Keychange is ambitiously taking multiple actions for gender equality. It is timely, situated in contemporary media debates about gendered representation and other inequalities affecting music festivals. Hinderances to its success can be the money-making priorities of the music industries and the neoliberal governance of European nations and the EU.

Conclusion

Billie Eilish was featured on the cover of British *Vogue*'s June 2021 issue wearing a pink corset, blonde movie star hair, reminding the reader of Marilyn Monroe, with matching make-up, and a headline that read 'It's All about What Makes You Feel Good'. The photo was also shared by the artist on Instagram and that post broke Instagram's record for most likes ever. Besides being appreciated by her followers, the visual style the photo showed off, which was different from how Eilish looked in 2019 as discussed in Chapter 3, sparked a debate online. Some asked was she selling out, was she going to be like everyone else? Their use of 'everyone' implied young female entertainers and influencers complying with beauty industry ideals. Had money changed her, as some argued, made her less 'real', or was this a result of 'growth' in age and taste on her part? Billie Eilish herself spoke out against the negative comments. She defended her right to wear different looks and experiment with different styles, not just one, and to change the style and colour of her hair. Billie Eilish had previously spoken publicly about the media and fans policing her body, defending her right to not conform with beauty standards and not have her body and look be a matter of public debate – a feminist question indeed. It is a feminist question because of how women have been reduced to their bodies through history, because of the hard-won rights to decide over their own bodies, true especially for racialized groups. With the *Vogue* cover, her body was scrutinized again and the quality of her music was also put into question – being called a sell-out is not good for any artist. It is also noteworthy how being beautiful/beautified is contrasted with being a serious artist when her new style is deemed a 'sell-out'. The same month, her album *Happier Than Ever* was released thematizing fame, and not in an appealing way. Being constantly followed by paparazzi and stalkers is – for example – a violent experience of lack of privacy endured by Billie Eilish that the album addresses. The 'happiness' in the title can only be understood as ironic given the lyrics of the songs on the album.

Also in June 2021, the music video for the song 'Lost Cause' sparked another public discussion about Billie Eilish's sexual identity. In the music video, she is seen snuggling with a group of girls during what appears to be a slumber party, and in one of her Instagram posts she displayed a photo from the music video shoot and stated that she 'loves girls'. This led to speculation about her straight/queer/bi/lesbian identity, since Billie Eilish has previously said that she identifies as straight. It also led to her being accused of trying to attract queer fans without being queer. It was suggested that she was appropriating a queer identity to gain popularity with a queer fanbase, and she was accused of 'queer baiting'. The discussions around both the *Vogue* cover and the music video displayed with clarity that who Billie Eilish is, her self-identified gender and sexuality are interpreted as crucial for her political message. While her critique of body normativity, violent acts (like stalking) and toxic masculinity may be the same as before, her (possibly) changing artist persona alters how her feminism is understood in the discourse around feminism and gender politics in popular music.

Feminisms in popular music

The feminisms of mediated popular music studied in this book are very real even if not all of them have achieved societal or political results. Gender-based oppressions are challenged in mediated popular music, and social categories other than gender are critiqued together with gender for intersectional social justice to be achieved. For example, when 'Black woman' is used as a figure for social change by Beyoncé, or when Keychange challenges binary gender categories in the music industries by including several different gender options for artists, feminist ideas concerning gender and race permeate the popular music practice. The challenges to the status quo by feminisms in popular music can be directed at gender-based inequality in the music industries, or at inequality in the world in general, in private and in public. Neither Beyoncé nor Lady Gaga has invented new kinds of feminism, and Smirnoff and Spotify are not the first to implement integrating approaches from gender mainstreaming methodology to gender equality work in the business world. Feminist theories and methods that exist outside of popular music have been taken onboard and articulated in mediated popular music – the theoretical debates drawn upon precede the feminisms displayed in the empirical cases analysed in this book.

The influences of intersectional feminist discussions, understanding gender as always co-constructed with other sociocultural categories like sexuality, class and race, on the examples discussed in this book are strong. In the 2010s, feminist expressions in popular music often included showing diversity in terms of sexuality and race/ethnicity when a message of female empowerment, gender equality or women's rights was delivered. Feminist popular music artists speak out not only for women, but also for diversity and against racism and homophobia. Showing not only white women, straight women, skinny women, and also women (visually obvious) of more than one religion, Black and brown women, different body sizes, transwomen and people gendered outside the gender binary has been adopted as a way of doing feminism in popular music and popular culture. Despite the display of diversity questions concerning gender, race/ethnicity and sexuality can be addressed separately. For example, sexual harassment tends to become a 'women's' issue in popular music, racism an issue concerning 'Black' artists where other artists can be allies, and racist sexual harassment disappears in such a division (whoever is suffering from it). Despite such tendencies, there are also many examples of how several sociocultural categories are addressed by the same artist and in the same efforts, as shown clearly in Chapter 1. The intersectional turn of feminism in mediated popular music is not uncontested, but proved to be a popular feminism in the 2010s. The intersectional feminist influence on feminism in popular music translates into alliances with organizations outside of music, furthering intersectional feminist issues in society. One-question campaigns (for marriage equality or against sexual harassment and sexual violence) are one example, but feminist popular music artists have supported a diverse range of organizations, big and small, national and international, from Oxfam, the Women to Drive movement, to Black Lives Matter and the Democratic Party. Speaking and singing like a feminist are not enough to change the structural conditions and political realities of gender inequality, but the feminist discourse of the 2010s is translating into engagement in structural political change by popular music artists. At the same time, in feminist formulations of demands and complaints, it is difficult to shake the idea that some oppressions are products of a gender-binary world, where the categories 'man' and 'woman' are overruling all other power trajectories, and where men are exposing women to violence. In #MeToo activism, the idea of a unified category of 'women' affected by sexual harassment and sexual violence can be the result, though the music industry petition analysed in the book presents a more complex picture on closer examination. Simplification is rhetorically effective, but if used as the base for suggestions for social change, it is insufficient to simplify power.

The second feminist tendency identified in this book is that an integrating approach to gender equality work has gained support in the music industries. The integrating approach to gender equality work (Squires 2005) acknowledges gender inequality and male domination in organizations and proposes a solution. According to the integrating approach, if the same number of women as men were included at all levels of decision-making, gender equality would be achieved. Such a thought has shaped both the equalizer and the original Keychange 2017–18 project. Combining an integrating approach to gender equality work with intersectional feminism is difficult to do. The integrating approach focuses on women and men, without further complicating power or addressing other sociocultural categories. It is hard to put the co-creation of sociocultural categories and power in focus when 'women' are treated as one group. Still, arguing that the music industries are male dominated, that it is unfair and needs to change, has proven effective in provoking policy change and reactions from decision-makers. This is probably working because the music industries in general have such very low numbers of female participants. The co-existence of intersectional feminism and integrating gender equality feminism is a rhetoric dilemma in the feminist discourse of popular music in the 2010s. According to the integrating approach, the numbers of women in boardrooms and on stages in the music industries hold the key to the end-of-gender oppression. Qualitative research on music industry agents that have achieved gender-balanced numbers has shown that gender inequality still exists in those organizations (Raine 2020), proving that gender oppression does not stop because women take their place on stage or in the studio. At odds with each other as they are both intersectional feminism and integrating gender equality feminism are the two strongest influences from feminist theories and methods in mediated popular music.

Mediated feminisms

The third tendency in 2010s popular music feminism that needs to be highlighted is the role that social media and other internet-based means, like music/film/television streaming services, spreading and discussing feminist messages have had on the popularity of feminism. The virality of social media and of the issues, that strongly polarize people writing on social media, makes feminism visible and therefore feminism is (always) co-existing with misogyny online (Banet-Weiser 2018), and where such debates occur racism, homophobia and transphobia often follow. The heightened emotions of people debating feminism online are producing a lot of content – positive and negative – that have given feminist artists a boost in publicity. Media can be the site of 'affective publics' whose views are translatable to social and political change through the use of social media and viral, transmedia practices (Papacharissi 2015), but an affective public may not be pro-feminist.

Much-talked about music videos are also much-watched music videos on YouTube. Social media, video sharing sites and streaming services also put more (if not all) control in the hands of artists during the 2010s. They have also provided artists with more easily accessible material to sample or use to further the feminist/anti-racist/ lesbian, gay, bisexual, transgender, queer and others (LGBTQ+) friendly politics. One much-discussed example is Beyoncé's sampling of YouTuber Messy Mya in the introduction of 'Formation'. Including a queer southern vlogger in a profile song by Beyoncé adds meaning, an alliance if you will, between her and southern queer culture in the United States. However, some saw it as opportunistic and even stealing rather than an alliance and a celebration.

During the 2010s, mainstream popular music artists adopted social media and now have greater control over the images and stories about them that are disseminated around the world. It is noteworthy that circulation and readership of *Vogue* are both below 1 million and the Billie Eilish *Vogue* cover received 17 million likes when she shared it on Instagram. The direction that feminist debates are taking in popular music is not easy to control, and neither are the effects those debates may have on an artist's career. Social media has changed the debate, discursively new actors like streaming services and online tabloid-like influencers further spread diverse images of and discuss popular music's feminisms. The mediation of feminism in popular music in this book happens across media, social media, streaming services, commercial media houses and video sharing sites that are all co-creating popular music's feminism.

Gender politics

When intersectional feminism and integrating gender equality feminism take part in mediated popular music, it is unavoidable that ideas and discussions about gender do so too. The femininity in the images of feminist artists has been debated, their bodies, their clothes, their love lives, their hair and make-up, if they are 'divas' or not. How they express their material and discursive gender plays a part in how their feminist politics are interpreted in discussions. When Billie Eilish changes her style, clothes, hair and make-up, the quality of her work and her political alliances with feminist, female and queer social groups are up for debate as well. In *Gaga: Five Foot Two*, Lady Gaga strives for a more serious artist persona and image. She is putting on a new (metaphorical and actual) costume and does so with new music, a new style and new types of projects. Your style, age and type of femininity affect the meaning of your political message. This is not a new argument in popular music. Researchers of Madonna discussed her reinventions of herself and her adaptation of contemporary feminist political themes in the 1990s (Schwichtenberg 1993). While some femininities are associated with some politics, femininity is needed to perform feminist politics in popular music. Few examples of persons gendered without femininity are expressing feminist views in the examples in this book.[1] Discussions about the personas and images of artists gendered feminine, their feminist views and interventions, and their persons are hard to keep apart.

Feminisms expressed in mainstream popular music in the 2010s have, as a larger discourse, interplayed with changing boundaries of gender expressions of femininity, transgender expressions and non-binary gendered

---

[1] Dj Honey Dijon is regarded as representing Black femininity, a woman, a transwoman and a person gendered feminine. Of course, male popular music artists can be feminists, like John Legend, and speak out. That is a topic in need of further research, not in focus here.

representation within popular music. The gendered representations in popular music's mainstream have widened than ever before in the 2010s to include more options for women, transgender and non-binary artists, more options for Black and brown artists and artists (openly) outside the heterosexual norm. More bodies of different sizes and shapes are represented in mainstream popular music videos and on stage, more roles are taken on and previously taboo topics have been raised. Some examples of these changes are as follows: successful female pop artists can be older; women, transgender and non-binary people are encouraged to produce and take on more diverse roles in the music industries; openly LGBTQ+ artists have entered the charts; sexual harassment is called out; racism and sexism in the music industries can be openly challenged; and Black and brown artists are growing in numbers in the charts (Smith et al. 2021). Feminism in popular music's mainstream in the 2010s has not resulted in the end-of-gender oppression in the music industries, nor the end of racism, transphobia or homophobia, but the artist representations are increasingly diverse, and the conversation about feminism is clearly articulated in the open as it has never been before.

Where to now?

The 2010s are over and the material this book builds on is in the past. What will happen to feminisms in the mainstream of mediated popular music in the decades to come? What potential to change the music industries to be less sexist, racist, homophobic or transphobic do the feminisms expressed in popular music in the 2010s contain? Can they be translated to structural and political change for a more (gender) equal world, and more equal working conditions for all working in music?[2] As discussed, some of the feminist interventions in this book have limited potential impact on gender-based oppression and should be critiqued for their lack of efficiency in fulfilling their

---

[2] Recent reports on racism in the UK music industries by Black lives in music (2021) establishes that racism affects artists as well as people with other positions in the industries.

aspirations. The equalizer's short period of equalizing listeners on Spotify has not changed careers, incomes or female artists' experiences of the music industries. It remains to be seen if the EQUAL hub will have such an impact.

Critiquing the intersectional interplay of gender, class and race and how it affects our social and cultural world is the cornerstone of intersectional feminist theory as formulated by Kimberlé Crenshaw (1991). She has argued that in political intersectionality, oppressions on these three grounds must be fought together, as co-constructed in societal structure. Social change cannot be achieved by ignoring the co-construction of these oppressions, according to Crenshaw. She is far from the only feminist theorist to argue the importance of an analysis of how capitalism operates to understand oppressions of gender and race. Donna Haraway (1991: 166–7) argues that the new transnational capitalist economy made possible by technological advances has created the 'homework' economy where stable jobs are rare and the gendered and racialized relations within and between countries has been affected. Following Haraway, promoting feminism and anti-racism without investigating capitalism and the work behind the scenes is a limited approach. For example: What are the effects for gender and race of big tech companies becoming more powerful in popular music? Nick Seaver's (2021) investigation of the white men behind the algorithms of music streaming suggests that the work structure of new capital, new workplaces, in the music industries does not promote gender equality and diversity.

When intersectional feminist ideas are adopted in mainstream popular culture, issues of class, capitalism, and the structure of work are omitted. According to Timothy Taylor (2016), capitalism and class oppression are rarely discussed in the research field studying popular music even though capitalism has been instrumental in shaping the music industries in the twentieth century. Popular music itself is defined by Roy Shuker (2017) as being commercial – capitalism is thus implied in the definition.[3] Today, the production, distribution, consumption and marketing of popular music are

---

[3] This definition may not hold up in all parts of the world though with respect to post-socialist contexts and the popular music produced there.

shaped by neoliberal capitalism together with globalization, financialization and new technologies (Taylor 2016: 4). The feminist trends analysed in this book focus on intersectional power analysis in terms of gender, LGBTQ+ rights and anti-racism, as well as integrating gender equality feminism. None of these feminisms addresses the challenge of neoliberal capitalism or the influx of capital from technology businesses into the music industries, Netflix and Spotify, for example. Capitalism and tech companies need to be analysed and challenged to pursue social equality, generally and in the music industries.

While I was completing this book, Beyoncé and her husband Jay Z were participating in an advertisement campaign for Tiffany & Co. In one photo, Beyoncé wears a large and very expensive yellow diamond, with little account of its history or origin. Critique followed, for example the campaign was seen as supporting colonialism and white supremacy since the diamond trade is killing miners in Africa and the benefiting companies are owned by white men and were formed based on historical colonial agreements in Africa.[4] Capitalism's role in colonialism and ownership of companies dealing in luxury goods is well documented. Luxury goods are often flaunted in popular music without anyone asking who makes them, who owns the means of production and why. When feminism, diversity, anti-racism and the fight for LGBTQ+ rights take place in popular music capitalism, its history of colonialism, war crimes, etc., and its effects – class divisions, poverty and social injustices – need to be discussed. There is no way to understand racism and colonialism without addressing capitalism and the profit made from unequal global systems, and there is no way to understand sexism without understanding the devaluing of feminized labour in the world. Here lies a strength of the post-feminist critique of popular culture: market logics can be combined with (rather than uprooted by) the challenges of intersectional and integrating gender equality feminisms as they are interpreted in mainstream popular music.

When gender expressions in mainstream popular music expanded in the 2010s, economic inequality was covered up by other issues. Action for

---

[4] https://www.nbcnews.com/think/opinion/what-beyonc-s-tiffany-diamond-ad-campaign-really-selling-ncna1277912 (visited 15 September 2021)

body positivity and trans inclusivity, or solidarity with the Women to Drive movement would hold more potential if the conditions of economic disparity creating poverty and interplaying with issues of global imbalance, heath and work could be addressed too. What are the capitalist histories behind the low support for Saudi women's rights? Who is benefiting from poor (sometimes racialized) people in the United States and around the world eating bad food and becoming overweight, and being individually blamed for it? How is the beauty industry entangled in transphobia? A hope for feminisms in mediated popular music in the future is that they will come to examine how capital and global economic power inequality affect the social justice issues that are already on the agenda.

References

Ahmed, Sara (2012). *On Being Included: Racism and Diversity in Institutional Life*. Durham, NC: Duke University Press.

Ahmed, Sara (2017). *Living a Feminist Life*. Durham, NC: Duke University Press.

Alvarez, Sonia E. (1999). 'Advocating Feminism: The Latin American Feminist NGO "Boom"', *International Feminist Journal of Politics*, 1 (2), 181–209, doi:10.1080/146167499359880.

Anzaldúa, Gloria (1991). *Borderlands: The new Mestiza = La Frontera*. 1st edn. San Francisco: Aunt Lute Books.

Baade, Christina and Kristin McGee (2021). *Beyoncé in the World*. Middleton: Wesleyan University Press.

Bacchi, Carol Lee (2009). *Analysing Policy: What's the Problem Represented to be?* Frenchs Forest, NSW: Pearson.

Bain, Vick (2019). *Counting the Music Industry: The Gender gap. A Study of Music Inequality in the UK Music Industry*. Arts Council England. https://img1.wsimg.com/blobby/go/0f1af03e-1d6c-4b2f-a3fb-ffebb8cd6604/downloads/Counting%20the%20Music%20Industry%20summary%202019.pdf.

Baker, Andrea, Katrina Williams, and Usha M. Rodrigues (2020). '#metoo 2.0 to #meNOmore: Analysing Western Reporting About Sexual Violence in the Music Industry', *Journalism Practice*, 14 (2), 191–207, doi:10.1080/17512786.2019.1674683.

Baker, Sarah (2004). 'Pop in(to) the Bedroom: Popular Music in Pre-Teen Girls' Bedroom Culture', *European Journal of Cultural Studies*, 7 (1), 75–93. doi:10.1177/1367549404039861.

Baker, Sarah, Andy Bennett, and Jodie Taylor (eds) (2013). *Redefining Mainstream Popular Music*. New York: Routledge.

Banet-Weiser, Sarah (2018). *Empowered: Popular Feminism and Popular Misogyny*. Durham, NC: Duke University Press.

Banet-Weiser, Sarah (2018). 'Postfeminism and Popular Feminism', *Feminist Media Histories*, 4 (2), 152–6.

Banet-Weiser, Sarah, Rosalind Gill, and Catherine Rottenberg (2020). 'Postfeminism, Popular Feminism and Neoliberal Feminism?: Sarah Banet-Weiser, Rosalind Gill and Catherine Rottenberg in Conversation', *Feminist Theory*, 21 (1), 3–24.

Battersby, Christine (1989). *Gender and Genius: Towards a Feminist Aesthetics*. London: Women's Press.

Bayton, Mavis (1998). *Frock Rock: Women Performing Popular Music*. Oxford: Oxford University Press.

Beer, David (2017). 'The Social Power of Algorithms', *Information, Communication & Society*, 20 (1), 1–13, doi:10.1080/1369118X.2016.1216147.

Bishop, Sophie (2018). 'Anxiety, Panic and Self-optimization: Inequalities and the YouTube Algorithm', *Convergence*, 24 (1), 69–84. doi:10.1177/1354856517736978.

Bivens, Rena (2017). 'The Gender Binary Will not be Deprogrammed: Ten Years of Coding Gender on Facebook', *New Media & Society*, 19 (6), 880–98. doi:10.1177/1461444815621527.

Björck, Cecilia (2011). *Claiming Space: Discourses on Gender, Popular Music, and Social Change*. Diss. Göteborg: Göteborgs Universitet. http://hdl.handle.net/2077/24290.

Björck, Cecilia (2021). 'Music, Gender and Social Change: Contemporary Debates, Directions and Challenges', in Silje Valde Onsrud, Hilde Synnøve Blix, and Ingeborg Lunde Vestad (eds), *Gender Issues in Scandinavian Music Education: From Stereotypes to Multiple Possibilities*, 28–50. Oxon: Routledge.

Black Lives in Music (2021). *Being Black in the UK Music Industry*. https://blim.org.uk/report/report-9cpolsaz9uja/.

Blackstone, Amy, Jason Houle, and Christopher Uggen (2014). '"I Didn't Recognize it as a Bad Experience Until I was Much Older". Age, Experience, and Workers' Perceptions of Sexual Harassment', *Sociological Spectrum*, 34 (4), 314–37, doi:10.1080/02732173.2014.917247.

Bock, Jannika (2008). *Riot Grrrl. A Feminist Re-interpretation of the Punk Narrative*. Saarbrücken: VDM Verlag Dr. Müller.

Bonini, Tiziano and Alessandro Gandini (2019). "First Week Is Editorial, Second Week Is Algorithmic': Platform Gatekeepers and the Platformization of Music Curation', *Social Media + Society*, October, 1–11. https://doi.org/10.1177/2056305119880006.

Born, Georgina and David Hesmondhalgh (eds) (2000). *Western Music and Its Others: Difference, Representation, and Appropriation in Music*. Berkeley: University of California Press.

Braidotti, Rosi (2019). 'A Theoretical Framework for the Critical Posthumanities', *Theory, Culture & Society*, 36 (6), 31–61. doi:10.1177/0263276418771486.

Braun, Virginia and Victoria Clarke (2006). 'Using Thematic Analysis in Psychology', *Qualitative Research in Psychology*, 3 (2), 77–101, doi:10.1191/1478088706qp063oa.

Bridge, Simone Krüger (2020). 'Gendering Music in Popular Culture', in Karen Ross (ed.), *The International Encyclopedia of Gender, Media, and Communication*. New York: Wiley Blackwell.

Bucher, Taina (2018). *If...then: Algorithmic Power and Politics*. New York: Oxford University Press.

Burns, Lori (2002). *Disruptive Divas: Feminism, Identity, & Popular Music*. New York: Garland.

Butler, Judith (1990). *Gender Trouble: Feminism and the Subversion of Identity*. New York: Routledge.

Butler, Judith (2004). *Undoing Gender*. New York: Routledge.

Citron, Marcia J. (1993). *Gender and the Musical Canon*. Cambridge: Cambridge Univ. Press.

Cixous, Hélène (1976). 'The Laugh of Medusa', *Literary Theory: An Anthology*. 940–954.

Clark, Meredith D. (2020). 'DRAG THEM: A Brief Etymology of so-called "cancel Culture."', *Communication and the Public*, 5 (3–4), 88–92. doi:10.1177/2057047320961562.

Coase, R.H. (1979). 'Payola in Radio and Television Broadcasting', *The Journal of Law and Economics*, 22 (2), 269–328.

Coates, Norma (1998). 'Can't we Just Talk About Music?: Rock and Gender on the Internet', in Thomas Swiss, John M. Sloop and Andrew Herman (eds.), *Mapping the Beat: Popular Music and Contemporary Theory*, Malden: Blackwell, 77–99.

Colbjørnsen, Terje (2020). 'The Streaming Network: Conceptualizing Distribution Economy, Technology, and Power in Streaming Media Services', *Convergence*. October. doi:10.1177/1354856520966911.

Coleman, Claire (2017). 'Voicing Experience: Female Indie Musicians "calling out" Sexism', *Feminist Media Studies*, 17 (1), 121–5, doi:10.1080/14680777.2017.1261466.

Collins, Patricia Hill (1998). 'It's all in the Family. Intersections of Gender, Race and Nation', *Hypatia*, 13 (3), 62–82.

Cooper, Elizabeth Whittington (2016). 'Sex(uality), Marriage, Motherhood and 'Bey Feminism', in Adrienne M. Trier-Bieniek (ed.), *The Beyoncé Effect: Essays on Sexuality, Race and Feminism*, 203–14. Jefferson, NC: McFarland & Company, Inc., Publishers.

Crenshaw, Kimberlé (1991). 'Mapping the Margins: Intersectionality, Identity Politics and Violence Against Women of Color', *Stanford Law Review*, 43 (6), 1241–99.

Crider, David (2020). 'Of "Tomatoes" and Men: A Continuing Analysis of Gender in Music Radio Formats', *Journal of Radio & Audio Media*, 27 (1), 134–50, doi:10.1080/19376529.2019.1623221.

Dagens Nyheter (2017): '#närmusikentystnar. Jag Vågade Aldrig Berätta – då Skulle jag Inte få Sjunga', 18th of November 2017 (#whenthemusicgoessilent I Never Dared to Tell – Then I Wouldn't get to Sing').

Dankić, Andrea (2019). *Att Göra Hiphop: En Studie av Musikpraktiker och Sociala Positioner*. Diss. Stockholm : Stockholms Universitet. (Making Hiphop: A Study of Musical Practices and Social Positions).

Davis, Angela Yvonne (1998). *Blues Legacies and Black Feminism: Gertrude "Ma" Rainey, Bessie Smith, and Billie Holiday*. New York: Pantheon Books.

De Boise, Sam (2019). 'Gender Mainstreaming in the Music Industries: Perspectives From Sweden and the UK', in Sarah Raine and Catherine Strong (eds), *Towards Gender Equality in the Music Industry: Education, Practice and Strategies for Change*, 117–30. New York: Bloomsbury Academic.

De Laat, Kim (2019). 'Singing the Romance: Gendered and Racialized Representations of Love and Postfeminism in Popular Music'. *Poetics*, 77, 1–14.

De Lauretis, Teresa (1987). *Technologies of Gender: Essays on Theory, Film, and Fiction*. Bloomington: Indiana University Press.

D'Ignazio, Catherine and Lauren F. Klein (2020). *Data Feminism*. Cambridge, MA: The MIT Press.

Dijck, José van (2013). *The Culture of Connectivity: A Critical History of Social Media*. New York: Oxford University Press.

Dow, Bonnie J. (1996). *Prime-time Feminism: Television, Media Culture, and the Women's Movement Since 1970*. Philadelphia: University of Pennsylvania Press.

Drott, Eric (2020). 'Fake Streams, Listening Bots and Click Farms: Counterfeiting Attention in the Streaming Music Economy', *American Music*, 38 (2), 153–75.

Durham, Aisha S. (2014). *Home With hip hop Feminism: Performances in Communication and Culture*. New York: Peter Lang Publishing Inc.

Edelman, Lee (2004). *No Future: Queer Theory and the Death Drive*. Durham, NC: Duke University Press.

Epps-Darling, Avriel, Romain Takeo Bouyer, and Henrietta Cramer (2020). 'Artist Gender Representation in Music Streaming', *21st International Society for Music Information Retrieval Conference*, Montréal, Canada. https://program.ismir2020.net/static/final_papers/148.pdf.

Eriksson, Maria and Anna Johansson (2017). 'Tracking Gendered Streams', *Culture Unbound*, 9 (2), 163–83. https://doi.org/10.3384/cu.2000.1525.1792163.

Eriksson, Maria, Rasmus Fleischer, Anna Johansson, Pelle Snickars, and Patrick Vonderau (2019). *Spotify Teardown: Inside the Black box of Streaming Music*. Cambridge, MA: MIT Press.

Erlingsdóttir, Irma and Chandra Giti (eds) (2021). *The Routledge Handbook of the Politics of the #MeToo Movement*. Milton Park, Abingdon, Oxon: Routledge.

Farrugia, Rebekah and Kellie D. Hay (2020). *Women Rapping Revolution: Hip hop and Community Building in Detroit*. Oakland: University of California Press.

Fast, Susan and Craig Jennex (eds) (2019). *Popular Music and the Politics of Hope: Queer and Feminist Interventions*. New York: Routledge.

Felski, Rita (2015). *The Limits of Critique*. Chicago, IL: University of Chicago Press.

Fileborn, Bianca, Phillip Wadds, and Stephen Tomsen (2020). 'Sexual Harassment and Violence at Australian Music Festivals: Reporting Practices and Experiences of Festival Attendees', *Australian & New Zealand Journal of Criminology*, 53 (2), 194–212. doi:10.1177/0004865820903777.

Gadir, Tami (2017). 'Forty-seven DJs, Four Women: Meritocracy, Talent and Postfeminist Politics', *Dancecult: Journal of Electronic Dance Music Culture*, 9 (1), 50–72, doi:10.12801/1947-5403.2017.09.01.03.

Galloway, Alexander R. (2006). *Gaming: Essays on Algorithmic Culture*. Minneapolis: University of Minnesota Press.

Giffort, Danielle M. (2011). 'Show or Tell? Feminist Dilemmas and Implicit Feminism at Girls' Rock Camp', *Gender & Society*, 25 (5), 569–88. doi:10.1177/0891243211415978.

Gill, Rosalind (2007). *Gender and the Media*. Cambridge: Polity.

Gill, Rosalind (2016). 'Post-postfeminism?: New Feminist Visibilities in Postfeminist Times', *Feminist Media Studies*, 16 (4), 610–30.

Gill, Rosalind (2017). 'The Affective, Cultural and Psychic Life of Postfeminism: A Postfeminist Sensibility 10 Years On', *European Journal of Cultural Studies*, 20 (6), 606–26. https://doi.org/10.1177/1367549417733003.

Goldman, Robert (1992). *Reading ads Socially*. London: Routledge.

Green, Lucy (1997). *Music, Gender, Education*. Cambridge: Cambridge University Press.

Grosz, Elizabeth (1995). *Space, Time, and Perversion: Essays on the Politics of Bodies*. New York: Routledge.

Grubbström, Ann and Stina Powell (2020). 'Persistent Norms and the #MeToo Effect in Swedish Forestry Education', *Scandinavian Journal of Forest Research*, 35 (5–6), 308–18, doi:10.1080/02827581.2020.1791243.

Halberstam, Judith (2012). *Gaga Feminism: Sex, Gender, and the end of Normal*. Boston: Beacon Press.

Halberstam, Jack (2021). 'Weiners, Whiners, Weinsteins, and Worse', in Irma Erlingsdóttir and Chandra Giti (eds), *The Routledge Handbook of the Politics of the #MeToo Movement*. Milton Park, Abingdon, Oxon: Routledge, 182–6..

Hall, Stuart (ed) (1997). *Representation: Cultural Representations and Signifying Practices*. London: Sage.

Hallinan, Blake and Ted Striphas (2016). 'Recommended for You: The Netflix Prize and the Production of Algorithmic Culture'. *New Media & Society*, 18 (1), 117–37. https://doi.org/10.1177/1461444814538646.

Hamer, Laura (2021). *The Cambridge Companion to Women in Music Since 1900*. New York: Cambridge University Press.

Hansson, Karin, Malin Sveningsson, and Hillevi Ganetz (2021). 'Organizing Safe Spaces: #MeToo Activism in Sweden', *Computer Supported Cooperative Work*, https://doi.org/10.1007/s10606-021-09410-7.

Haraldsdóttir, Freyja (2021). 'Being a Disabled Feminist Killjoy in a Feminist Movement', in Irma Erlingsdóttir and Chandra Giti (eds), *The Routledge Handbook of the Politics of the #MeToo Movement*, 221–30. Milton Park, Abingdon, Oxon: Routledge.

Haraway, Donna Jeanne (1991). *Simians, Cyborgs, and Women: The Reinvention of Nature*. London: Free Association Books.

Hawkins, Stan (ed) (2017). *The Routledge Research Companion to Popular Music and Gender'*. Abingdon, Oxon, New York: Routledge.

Hayles N. Katherine (1999). *How we Became Posthuman: Virtual Bodies in Cybernetics, Literature, and Informatics*. Chicago, IL: University of Chicago Press.

Hemmings, Clare (2012). 'Affective Solidarity: Feminist Reflexivity and Political Transformation', *Feminist Theory*, 13 (2), 147–61. doi:10.1177/1464700112-442643.

Hill, Rosemary Lucy (2016). *Gender, Metal and the Media: Women Fans and the Gendered Experience of Music*. London: Palgrave Macmillan.

Hill, Rosemary Lucy, David Hesmondhalgh, and Molly Megson (2020). 'Sexual Violence at Live Music Events: Experiences, Responses and Prevention', *International Journal of Cultural Studies*, 23 (3), 368–84. doi:10.1177/1367877919891730.

hooks, Bell (1984). *Feminist Theory From Margin to Center*. Boston, MA: South End Press.

Hsu, V. Jo (2019). '(Trans)forming #MeToo: Toward a Networked Response to Gender Violence', *Women's Studies in Communication*, 42 (3), 269–86, doi:10.1080/07491409.2019.1630697.

James, Robin (2015). *Resilience & Melancholy: Pop Music, Feminism, Neoliberalism*. Winchester: Zero Books.

James, Robin (2017). 'Is the Post- in Post-identity the Post- in Post-genre?', *Popular Music*, 36 (1), 21–32. doi:10.1017/S0261143016000647.

James, Robin (2020). 'Music and Feminism in the 21st Century', *Music Research Annual*, 1, 1–25. https://musicresearchannual.org/wp-content/uploads/2021/01/jamese28094music-and-feminism.pdf.

Jeffreys, Sheila (2009). 'Prostitution, Trafficking and Feminism: An Update on the Debate', *Women's Studies International Forum*, 32, 316–20. doi:10.1016/j.wsif.2009.07.002.

Jenkins, Henry, Sam Ford, and Joshua Green (2013). *Spreadable Media: Creating Value and Meaning in a Networked Culture*. New York: New York University Press.

Johansson, Sofia, Ann Werner, Patrik Åker, and Gregory Goldenzwaig (eds.) (2017). *Streaming Music: Practices, Media, Cultures*. Abingdon, Oxon: Routledge.

Kagal, Neha, Leah Cowan, and Huda Jawad (2019). 'Beyond the Bright Lights: Are Minoritized Women Outside the Spotlight Able to Say #MeToo?', in Bianca Fileborn and Rachel Loney-Howes (eds), *#MeToo and the Politics of Social Change*. Cham: Palgrave Macmillan. https://doi.org/10.1007/978-3-030-15213-0_9.

Kearney, Mary Celeste (2017). *Gender and Rock*. New York: Oxford University Press.

Keychange PRS Foundation (2018). *Keychange Manifesto: Recommendations for a Balanced Music Industry*. https://static1.squarespace.com/static/5e3ac2fecd69e2663a9b793c/t/5f0324b481fcf002f4f702c9/1594041527239/1052-keychange-A5-v15-web.pdf.

King, Nigel and Christine Horrocks (2010). *Interviews in Qualitative Research*. Los Angeles: Sage.

Krogh, Mads (2020). "Context is the new Genre' Abstraktion og Singularisering i Digital Musikformidling', *Norsk Medietidskrift*, 27 (3), 1–15, https://doi.org/10.18261/ISSN.0805-9535-2020-03-05.

Kuhn, Annette (1982). *Women's Pictures: Feminism and Cinema*. London: Routledge & Kegan Paul.

Leonard, Marion (2007). *Gender in the Music Industry: Rock, Discourse and Girl Power*. Aldershot: Ashgate.

Leung, Rebecca and Robert Williams (2019). '#MeToo and Intersectionality: An Examination of the #MeToo Movement Through the R. Kelly Scandal', *Journal of Communication Inquiry*, 43 (4), 349–71. doi:10.1177/0196859919874138.

Lewis, Lisa A. (1990). *Gender Politics and MTV: Voicing the Difference*. Philadelphia: Temple University Press.

Li, Xinling (2019). *Black Masculinity and hip-hop Music. Black gay men who rap*. Singapore: Palgrave Macmillan.

Lieb, Kristin (2013). *Gender, Branding, and the Modern Music Industry: The Social Construction of Female Popular Music Stars*. New York: Routledge.

Lotz, Amanda D. (2001). 'Postfeminist Television Criticism: Rehabilitating Critical Terms and Identifying Postfeminist Attributes', *Feminist Media Studies*, 1 (1), 105–21, doi:10.1080/14680770120042891.

Lykke, Nina (2010). *Feminist Studies: A Guide to Intersectional Theory, Methodology and Writing*. New York: Routledge.

Marshall, Lee (2015). ""Let's Keep Music Special. F—Spotify': On-demand Streaming and the Controversy Over Artist Royalties', *Creative Industries Journal*, 8 (2), 177–89.

McClary, Susan (1991). *Feminine Endings: Music, Gender, and Sexuality*. Minneapolis: University of Minnesota Press.

McNeil, Maureen (2007). *Feminist Cultural Studies of Science and Technology*. London: Routledge.

McRobbie, Angela (2004). 'Notes on Postfeminism in Popular Culture. Bridget Jones and the new Gender Regime', in Anita Harris (ed.), *All About the Girl: Culture, Power, and Identity*, 3–14. New York: Routledge.

McRobbie, Angela (2007). 'Top Girls? Young Women and the Post-feminist Sexual Contract', *Cultural Studies*, 21 (4–5), 718–37, doi:10.1080/09502380701279044.

McRobbie, Angela (2009). *The Aftermath of Feminism: Gender, Culture and Social Change*. London: Sage.

Mendes, Kaitlynn, Jessica Ringrose, and Jessalynn Keller (2018). '#MeToo and the Promise and Pitfalls of Challenging Rape Culture Through Digital Feminist Activism', *European Journal of Women's Studies*, 25 (2), 236–46. doi:10.1177/135050681-8765318.

Millett, Kate (1970). *Sexual Politics*. New York: Garden City.

Moseley, Rachel and Jacinda Read (2002). '"Having it Ally": Popular Television (Post-) Feminism', *Feminist Media Studies*, 2 (2), 231–49. doi:10.1080/14680770220150881.

Muchitsch, Veronika (2020). *Vocal Figurations: Technique, Technology, and Mediation in the Gendering of Voice in Twenty-first-century pop Music*. Diss. Uppsala: Uppsala University.

Müller, L.J. (2017). 'Hearing Sexism – Analyzing Discrimination in Sound', in Julia Merrill (ed.), *Popular Music Studies Today*, 225–34. Systematische Musikwissenschaft. Wiesbaden: Springer VS.

Murray, Dara Persis (2013). 'Branding "real" Social Change in Dove's Campaign for Real Beauty', *Feminist Media Studies*, 13 (1), 83–101, doi:10.1080/14680777.2011.647963.

Noble, Safiya (2018). *Algorithms of Oppression: How Search Engines Reinforce Racism*. New York: New York University Press.

Onwuachi-Willig, Angela (2018). 'What About #UsToo: The Invisibility of Race in the #MeToo Movement', *The Yale Law Journal Forum*, 128, 105–20.

Papacharissi, Zizi (2012). 'Without you, I'm Nothing: Performances of the Self on Twitter', *International Journal of Communication*, 6, 1989–2006.

Papacharissi, Zizi (2015). *Affective Publics: Sentiment, Technology, and Politics*. Oxford: Oxford University Press.

Pollock, Griselda (1999). *Differencing the Canon: Feminist Desire and the Writing of Art's Histories*. London: Routledge.

Potter, Jonathan and Margaret Wetherell (1987). *Discourse and Social Psychology: Beyond Attitudes and Behaviour*. London: Sage.

Prey, Robert (2020). 'Locating Power in Platformization: Music Streaming Playlists and Curatorial Power', *Social Media + Society*. April-June, 1–11, doi:10.1177/2056305120933291.

Propst, Paula Danielle (2017). *Sonic Feminism: Intentionality, Empathy, and Emotions at Rock and Roll Camps*. Diss. University of California Riverside, Diss. https://escholarship.org/uc/item/2fc9f1xj.

Prügl, Elisabeth (2011). 'Diversity Management and Gender Mainstreaming as Technologies of Government', *Politics and Gender*, 7 (1), 71–89.

Raine, Sarah (2020). *Keychanges at Cheltenham Jazz Festival: Challenges for Women Musicians in Jazz and Ways Forward for Equal Gender Representation at Jazz Festivals*. doi:10.13140/RG.2.2.15390.15688.

Raine, Sarah and Catherine Strong (eds) (2019). *Towards Gender Equality in the Music Industry: Education, Practice and Strategies for Change*. New York: Bloomsbury Academic

Reddington, Helen (2021). *She's at the Controls: Sound Engineering, Production and Gender Ventriloquism in the 21st Century*. Bristol: Equinox Publishing Ltd.

Ringrose, Jessica and Valerie Walkerdine (2008). 'Regulating The Abject', *Feminist Media Studies*, 8 (3), 227–46, doi:10.1080/14680770802217279.

Rottenberg, Catherine (2014). 'The Rise of Neoliberal Feminism', *Cultural Studies*, 28 (3), 418–37, doi:10.1080/09502386.2013.857361.

Rottenberg, Catherine (2018). *The Rise of Neoliberal Feminism*. New York: Oxford University Press.

Scharff, Christina (2015). 'Blowing Your own Trumpet: Exploring the Gendered Dynamics of Self-Promotion in the Classical Music Profession', *The Sociological Review*, 63 (1), 97–112. doi:10.1111/1467-954X.12243.

Schilt, Kristen (2003). "A Little too Ironic': The Appropriation and Packaging of Riot Grrrl Politics by Mainstream Female Musicians', *Popular Music and Society*, 26 (1), 5–16, doi:10.1080/0300776032000076351.

Schwichtenberg, Cathy (ed) (1993). *The Madonna Connection: Representational Politics, Subcultural Identities and Cultural Theory*. Boulder: Westview P., U. S.

Scoular, Jane (2004). 'The 'subject' of Prostitution: Interpreting the Discursive, Symbolic and Material Position of sex/work in Feminist Theory', *Feminist Theory*, 5 (3), 343–55. doi:10.1177/1464700104046983.

Seaver, Nick (2021). 'Seeing Like an Infrastructure: Avidity and Difference in Algorithmic Recommendation', *Cultural Studies*, 35 (4–5), 771–91, doi:10.1080/09502386.2021.1895248.

Sedgwick, Eve Kosofsky (2003). *Touching Feeling: Affect, Pedagogy, Performativity*. Durham, NC: Duke University Press.

Shuker, Roy (2017). *Popular Music: The Key Concepts*, 4th edn. Oxon: Routledge.

Smith, Stacey L., Katherine Pieper, Marc Choueiti, Karla Hernandez, and Kevin Yao (2021). *Inclusion in the Recording Studio? Gender and Race/Ethnicity of Artists, Songwriters and Producers Across 600 Popular Songs From 2012-2020*. California: Annenberg Inclusion Initiative, University of Southern California. https://assets.uscannenberg.org/docs/aii-inclusion-recording-studio2021.pdf.

Sobande, Fransesca (2021). 'Spectacularized and Branded Digital (Re)presentations of Black People and Blackness', *Television & New Media*, 22 (2), 131–46. doi:10.1177/1527476420983745.

Squires, Judith (2005). 'Is Mainstreaming Transformative? Theorizing Mainstreaming in the Context of Diversity and Deliberation', *Social Politics: International Studies in Gender, State & Society*, 12 (3), 366–88, https://doi.org/10.1093/sp/jxi020.

Striphas, Ted (2015). 'Algorithmic Culture'. *European Journal of Cultural Studies*, 18 (4–5), 395–412. https://doi.org/10.1177/1367549415577392.

Strong, Catherine and Emma Rush (2018). 'Musical Genius and/or Nasty Piece of Work? Dealing With Violence and Sexual Assault in Accounts of Popular Music's Past', *Continuum*, 32 (5), 569–80, doi:10.1080/10304312.2018.1483009.

Sundén, Jenny (2015). 'On Trans-, Glitch, and Gender as Machinery of Failure', *First Monday*, 20 (4). http://firstmonday.org/ojs/index.php/fm/article/view/5895/4416.

Sundén, Jenny (2016). 'Glitch, Genus, Tillfälligt Avbrott: Femininitet som Trasighetens Teknologi', *Lambda Nordica*, 2016 (1–2), 23–45. (Glitch, Gender, Temporary Unavailable: Femininity as Broken Technology).

Sundén, Jenny and Susanna Paasonen (2020). *Who's Laughing Now? : Feminist Tactics in Social Media*. Cambridge, MA: MIT Press.

Susdorf, Marek (2017). 'Björk's Biophilia: A Musical Introduction to Feminist New Materialism', *Junctions: Graduate Journal of the Humanities*, 2 (2), 113–26. http://doi.org/10.33391/jgjh.39.

Svensson, Malin (2020). 'Sexuellt Trakasserad på Jobbet', *En Nordisk Forskningsöversikt*. Nordiska Ministerrådet. File:///Users/shwran08/Downloads/Se

xuellt%20trakasserad%20pa%20jobbet%20-%20en%20nordisk%20forskningsover sikt%202020.pdf (Sexually Harrassed at Work. A Nordic Research Review.)

Tasker, Yvonne and Diane Negra (eds) (2007). *Interrogating Postfeminism: Gender and the Politics of Popular Culture*. Durham, NC: Duke University Press.

Taylor, Jodie (2012). *Playing it Queer: Popular Music, Identity and Queer Worldmaking*. Bern: Peter Lang.

Taylor, Timothy D. (2016). *Music and Capitalism: A History of the Present*. Chicago, IL: The University of Chicago Press.

Trier-Bieniek, Adrienne M. (ed) (2016). *The Beyoncé Effect: Essays on Sexuality, Race and Feminism*. Jefferson, NC: McFarland & Company, Inc., Publishers.

Vernallis, Carol (2013). *Unruly Media: YouTube, Music Video, and the new Digital Cinema*. New York: Oxford University Press.

Werner, Ann (2020a). 'The Smirnoff Equaliser, En Feministisk Medieintervention för Strömmad Musik?', *Norsk Medietidskrift*, 27 (3), 1–15, https://doi.org/10.18261/ISSN.0805-9535-2020-03-04.

Werner, Ann (2020b). 'Organizing Music, Organizing Gender: Algorithmic Culture and Spotify Recommendations', *Popular Communication*, 18 (1), 78–90, doi:10.1080/15405702.2020.1715980.

Whiteley, Sheila (2000). *Women and Popular Music: Sexuality, Identity and Subjectivity*. London: Routledge.

Whiteley, Sheila (2005). *Too Much too Young: Popular Music, age, and Gender*. Abingdon: Routledge.

Wolfe, Paula (2020). *Women in the Studio: Creativity, Control and Gender in Popular Music Production*. Abingdon, Oxon: Routledge.

Index

affect 13, 21, 41–8
    affective dissonance 44
    affective publics 53, 141
age 57–61
Ahmed, Sara 69, 84
algorithm 79, 83, 85–6
algorithmic culture 79–81
Apple Music 78
audiences 41–2, 44–6

Bacchi, Carol 110
Banet-Weiser, Sarah 9, 25, 141
Beyoncé 2, 10, 20, 29–30, 36
    and audiences 42
    and Black Southern culture 39–40
    and costume 37
    and Messy Mya 141
    and motherhood 29–30
Bucher, Taina 83, 88

canon 4–6, 77
capitalism 130, 136, 144–5
Cheltenham Jazz Festival 114–15
Crenshaw, Kimberlé 6, 41, 123, 144

DJ culture 119
Doja Cat 1, 7–8
Drake 96
Dr Luke 3, 19

education for gender equality 112–13
Eilish, Billie 79, 100–3, 137–8, 141
    and 'Bad guy' 102–3
    and sexual identity 138
    and *Vogue* cover 137
embodiment 4, 42, 44
emotion 10, 25, 30–1, 37, 42–3, 46–7

fake streams 92–4
Felski, Rita 43

feminism 2–4, 6–7, 21–6, 33, 43, 47–8,
    51–5, 89, 91, 112, 133, 138–40,
    see also post-feminism
    Black feminism 41–2, 50, 123
    and gender politics 103, 138
    intersectional feminism 7–8, 17,
        123, 139–40, 144
    liberal feminism 5, 11–12, 81–2, 111
    and politics/demands 44, 52, 71–4,
        129–30, 142
    post-humanist feminism 13, 80–1
    radical feminism 52–3
feminist algorithm studies 79–1
feminist policy analysis 110
feminist queer theory 7, 60–1

Gadir, Tami 119
gender 3–7
    and binary 81–3
    and identity 86, 123
    and politics 142
    and subject 51
gender mainstreaming 87–8, 115
    and integrating 87–8, 140
    and transformative 87
gender pay gap 129–30, 135
genius, musical 67–8
Gill, Rosalind 10, 24–5, 35, 37, 60
Girls Rock Camp Alliance 112
#GlobalFeminism 85–6
Grande, Ariana 101–3
Grosz, Elizabeth 4

Haraway, Donna 13, 144
Hemmings, Clare 44
Hill, Anita 52
Honey Dijon 89

identity 9, 86, 122–3, 128, 138
intersectionality 6–7, 123, 144

keychange   108–11

Lady Gaga   19, 32–3, 40, 44–5, 83, 138
   and Mark Ronson   40, 44
   and mental health   33
   and monster   45
   and physical health   37
Leonard, Marion   128, 135
LGBTQ+   3, 47, 82, 86, 143
   and intersectionality   141
   and rights   7, 20, 38–9, 44–6
Lil Naz X   98–9

McRobbie, Angela   9, 21, 23, 32–3, 38–9
Madonna   21, 45, 142
Malcom X   41–2
media technology   4, 12–13, 79–80, 93–4, 145
men in groups   63–4
#MeToo   49–55, 140
music documentaries   20–1
music festivals   40, 63, 108–10, 114
music industries   64, 73
   and gender equality   110
music streaming services   78–9
Musikcentrum Öst   108
#MuteRKelly   90–1

neo-materialism   13
Netflix   21, 47
networking   134–5
non-binary   10, 81, 91, 143

Paasonen, Susanna   53, 66
Papacharissi, Zizi   75
payola   94
policy   11, 50, 55, 71–4, 88, 110–11, 114, 129–31, 135
pop   85, 126
Popkollo   112
popular music   4
post-feminism   9–10, 23–6, 33, 38

   and neoliberal feminism   25
   and popular feminism   25
   and popular music   26
PRS Foundation   108
Prügl, Elizabeth   89

queer theory   7, 60–1

race   6–7
racism   41–2, 80
Raine, Sarah   114–15
rap   1, 3, 8, 96, 98–9, 112
rape   61–2
Reeperbahn music festival   108
reggaeton   100
R Kelly   68, 90
rock   8–9, 19, 42, 59, 111–12
Rottenberg, Catherine   25, 31
Rush, Emma   67

Saweetie   1, 7–8
Sedgwick, Eve Kosovsky   21, 43
sexism   41–2, 44–5, 60, 80
sexual harassment   2, 5, 49–52, 63–4, 71
sexual violence   5, 49–52, 71, 115
Smirnoff equalizing music   77
social media   4, 12, 34, 37, 52–5, 75, 141
Spotify   77–8
Squires, Judith   87–8, 115, 130
Strong, Catherine   67
subject position   61, 75–6
Sundén, Jenny   53, 66
Swift, Taylor
   and eating disorders   35
   and Kanye West   34
   and politics   38, 45–6
   and sexual assault   39

tidal   78

woman/women   5–7

www.ingramcontent.com/pod-product-compliance
Lightning Source LLC
Chambersburg PA
CBHW061840300426
44115CB00013B/2459